GRANADA TRAVEL GUIDE 2024

Unveiling the Treasures of Granada: Your Passport to Adventure, Culture

Bill Bryson

Copyright © 2024 by Bill Bryson. All rights reserved. No part of this book may be reproduced or transmitted in any form or by any means, electronic or mechanical, including photocopying, recording, or by any information storage and retrieval system, without written permission from the author, except for the inclusion of brief quotations in a review

TABLE OF CONTENTS

1.0 Introduction
1.1 Overview of Granada
1.2 Brief History and Culture
1.3 Why Visit Granada

2.0 Planning Your Trip
2.1 Best Time to Visit
2.2 Visa and Entry Requirements
2.3 Currency and Banking
2.4 Health and safety tips
2.5 Packing Essentials

3.0 Transportation
3.1 Getting to Granada
3.2 Getting Around Granada
3.3 Public Transportation

4.0 Accommodation

4.1 Luxury hotel
4.2 Budget-Friendly Options
4.3 Boutique Hotels
4.4 Airbnb and Vacation Rentals

5.0 Shopping Guide
5.1 Shopping mall
5.2 Local Markets
5.3 Unique Souvenirs

6.0 Cuisine and Dining
6.1 Local Granada Dishes
6.2 Popular Restaurants and Cafes
6.3 Street Food Experiences

7.0 Exploring Granada
7.1 Alhambra Palace
7.2 Generalife Gardens
7.3 Nasrid Palaces
7.4 Alcazaba Fortress
7.5 Granada Cathedral
7.6 Albayzín District

7.7 Sacromonte Caves
7.8 Royal Chapel of Granada
7.9 Science Park

8.0 Outdoor Adventures
8.1 Sierra Nevada National Park
8.2 Skiing and Snowboarding
8.3 Hiking Trails
8.4 Alpujarras Region
8.5 Villages Tour

9.0 Cultural Immersion
9.1 Flamenco Shows
9.2 Tapas Tours
9.3 Local Festivals
9.4 Corpus Christi Festival
9.5 Granada International Jazz Festival

10.0 Practical Tips
10.1 Language and Communication
10.2 Photography Etiquette

10.3 General emergency contact in Granada

11.0 Sample Itineraries
11.1 One Week Itinerary
11.2 Weekend Getaway
11.3 Budget Traveler's Guide

12.0 Conclusion

WELCOME NOTE

Welcome, Dear traveler, to the enchanting city of Granada! As you embark on your journey to this magical destination, let me extend a warm and heartfelt welcome to you. Whether you're a seasoned adventurer or a first-time explorer, Granada promises to captivate your senses, ignite your curiosity, and leave you with memories to cherish for a lifetime.

Picture yourself strolling through the historic streets of the Albayzín, where the echoes of centuries past mingle with the vibrant energy of modern-day Granada.

Imagine standing in awe before the majestic Alhambra Palace, its intricate architecture and lush gardens beckoning you to step back in time and immerse yourself in the splendor of Moorish Spain

But Granada is more than just its iconic landmarks – it's a city of hidden treasures waiting to be discovered. From cozy tapas bars serving up mouthwatering delicacies to bustling markets overflowing with local treasures, every corner of Granada holds a new adventure, a new story, a new experience waiting to unfold.

As you journey through Granada, let this travel guide be your trusted companion, your insider's guide to all the best that this city has to offer. Whether you're seeking recommendations for the perfect spot to watch the sunset, tips on where to find the best flamenco show in town, or advice on navigating the city like a local, we've got you covered.

So grab your map, lace up your walking shoes, and get ready to embark on the adventure of a lifetime in Granada. Whether you spend a day, a week, or a lifetime exploring this vibrant city, one thing is certain – you'll leave with a heart full of memories, a soul touched by the magic of Granada, and a longing to return again and again.

Welcome to Granada – where every moment is an opportunity for discovery, every street is a pathway to adventure, and every traveler is embraced like an old friend. Let the journey begin!

1.0 Introduction

1.1 Overview of Granada

Granada, located in the Andalusia region of southern Spain, is a city steeped in history, culture, and natural beauty. Nestled at the foot of the Sierra Nevada mountains, Granada boasts a rich heritage that blends Moorish, Christian, and Jewish influences, making it a captivating destination for travelers from around the world.

1. Historical Significance:

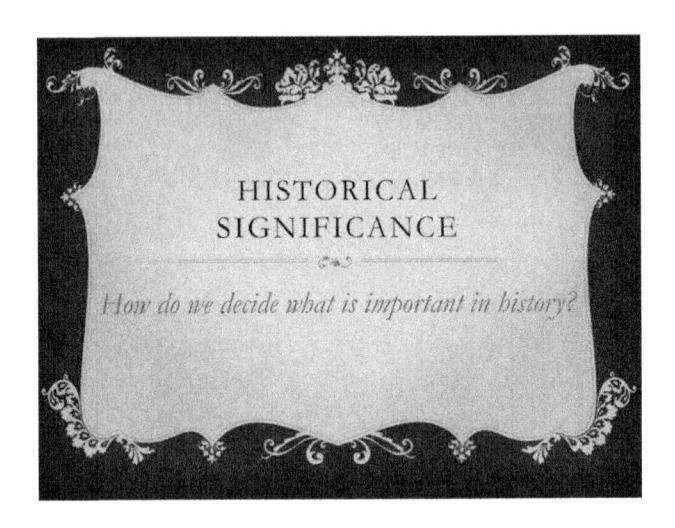

> **HISTORICAL SIGNIFICANCE**
> How do we decide what is important in history?

Granada's history dates back over two millennia, with evidence of human settlement from as early as the Neolithic period.

The city flourished under Moorish rule during the Islamic Golden Age and reached its zenith as the capital of the Emirate of Granada in the 13th century.

One of Granada's most iconic landmarks, the Alhambra Palace, was constructed during this period, serving as a royal residence and fortress for the Nasrid dynasty.

2. Architectural Marvels:

The Alhambra Palace stands as a testament to the architectural brilliance of Islamic

Spain, with its intricate stucco work, ornate tile patterns, and tranquil gardens.

Granada's historic center is a labyrinth of narrow streets and alleys, lined with centuries-old buildings adorned with wrought-iron balconies and colorful ceramic tiles.

The Albayzín district, a UNESCO World Heritage site, offers panoramic views of the Alhambra and showcases the city's Moorish heritage through its winding streets and traditional white-washed houses.

3. Cultural Fusion:

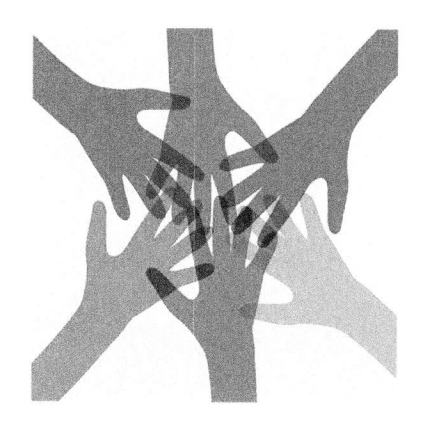

Granada's diverse cultural heritage is reflected in its vibrant arts scene, which encompasses flamenco music and dance, traditional Moorish crafts, and contemporary art exhibitions.

The city's culinary landscape is equally diverse, with influences from Arabic, Jewish, and Andalusian cuisines evident in its tapas bars, markets, and fine dining establishments.

Throughout the year, Granada hosts a variety of cultural festivals and events, including the International Festival of Music and Dance and the Festival of Corpus Christi, showcasing the city's rich cultural traditions.

4. Natural Beauty:

Beyond its historic attractions, Granada is blessed with breathtaking natural scenery, including the snow-capped peaks of the Sierra Nevada mountains and the lush valleys of the Alpujarras region.
Outdoor enthusiasts can explore the extensive network of hiking trails in the Sierra Nevada National Park, go skiing or

snowboarding in the winter months, or relax in the natural hot springs of the Alhama de Granada.

The city's strategic location between the mountains and the Mediterranean coast also offers opportunities for day trips to coastal towns such as Nerja and cultural excursions to nearby cities like Cordoba and Seville.

5. Modern Amenities:

Despite its ancient origins, Granada is a modern and cosmopolitan city, with world-class museums, universities, and research institutions.

The city's vibrant nightlife scene attracts students and young professionals from across Spain and beyond, with an array of bars, clubs, and live music venues catering to all tastes.

Granada's public transportation system is efficient and affordable, making it easy for visitors to explore the city and its surroundings without the need for a car.

In summary, Granada offers a unique blend of history, culture, and natural beauty that appeals to travelers seeking an authentic Spanish experience. Whether exploring the Alhambra Palace, savoring tapas in the Albayzín, or skiing in the Sierra Nevada, visitors to Granada are sure to be enchanted by its charm and allure.

1.2 Brief History and Culture

1. Ancient Origins:

Granada's history dates back thousands of years, with evidence of human settlement in the region dating to the Neolithic period.

The area was inhabited by various indigenous tribes, including the Iberians and the Celts, before coming under Roman rule in the 3rd century BCE.

Following the collapse of the Roman Empire, Granada was conquered by the Visigoths in the 5th century CE, marking the beginning of the city's Christian era.

2. Moorish Rule and the Golden Age:

Granada reached its zenith during the Islamic Golden Age when it served as the capital of the Emirate of Granada, one of the last Muslim kingdoms in Spain.

The most iconic symbol of this period is the Alhambra Palace, constructed in the 13th and 14th centuries by the Nasrid dynasty.

Under Moorish rule, Granada became a center of learning, art, and architecture, with advancements in science, mathematics, and literature.

3. Reconquista and Christian Rule:

The Catholic Monarchs, Queen Isabella I of Castile and King Ferdinand II of Aragon, completed the Reconquista with the capture of Granada in 1492, ending over seven centuries of Muslim rule in the Iberian Peninsula.
The fall of Granada marked the culmination of the Spanish Reconquista and the beginning of the Spanish Renaissance.
The Catholic Monarchs commissioned the construction of the Royal Chapel of Granada, where they are buried, and initiated the Christianization of the city.

4. Cultural Fusion:

The coexistence of Christians, Muslims, and Jews in Granada during the Middle Ages led to a rich cultural exchange, resulting in the blending of diverse artistic, architectural, and culinary traditions.

This cultural fusion is evident in the city's historic landmarks, such as the Alhambra, which features Islamic, Christian, and Jewish motifs, and the Albayzín district, with its labyrinthine streets and Moorish architecture.

5. Golden Age of Literature and Arts:

Granada was a hub of literary and artistic activity during the Renaissance, attracting poets, writers, and musicians from across Spain and Europe.

The city was home to prominent figures such as the poet and playwright Federico García Lorca and the composer Manuel de Falla, who drew inspiration from Granada's rich cultural heritage in their works.

6. Modern Era:

In the 20th century, Granada experienced significant social and political upheaval, including the Spanish Civil War and the subsequent dictatorship of Francisco Franco.

Despite this turmoil, Granada emerged as a center of academic excellence, with the founding of the University of Granada in 1531 and the establishment of research institutions and cultural organizations.

7. Contemporary Culture:

Today, Granada continues to celebrate its cultural heritage through festivals, concerts, and art exhibitions held throughout the year.
The city's vibrant flamenco scene, traditional tapas culture, and thriving arts community attract visitors from around the world, making Granada a dynamic and cosmopolitan destination.
In summary, Granada's history is a tapestry woven with the threads of diverse cultures and civilizations, each leaving its mark on the city's architecture, cuisine, and customs. From its ancient origins to its vibrant contemporary culture, Granada remains a testament to the enduring legacy of Spain's multicultural heritage.

1.3 Why Visit Granada

Granada, with its rich history, stunning architecture, vibrant culture, and breathtaking natural landscapes, offers a myriad of reasons for travelers to visit. Here are several compelling reasons why Granada should be on everyone's travel itinerary:

1. The Alhambra Palace:

Undoubtedly the crown jewel of Granada, the Alhambra Palace is a UNESCO World Heritage site and one of the most visited attractions in Spain.

This magnificent fortress-palace complex showcases exquisite Islamic architecture, intricate tile work, and lush gardens, offering visitors a glimpse into the opulence of Moorish Spain.

Highlights of the Alhambra include the Nasrid Palaces, Generalife Gardens, and the Alcazaba fortress, each boasting stunning architectural details and sweeping views of the city.

2. Historic Charm:

Granada's historic center is a labyrinth of narrow cobblestone streets, whitewashed buildings, and hidden plazas, where centuries of history are preserved around every corner.

The Albayzín district, with its medieval Moorish architecture and panoramic views of the Alhambra, is a UNESCO World Heritage site and a testament to Granada's multicultural heritage.

Other notable landmarks include the Granada Cathedral, Royal Chapel, and the Alcaicería market, where visitors can shop for traditional crafts and souvenirs.

3. Cultural Experiences:

Granada is a cultural melting pot, where Christian, Muslim, and Jewish traditions coexist and thrive.

Visitors can immerse themselves in the city's vibrant arts scene, attending flamenco shows, concerts, and theatrical performances held in historic venues.

Granada's culinary scene is equally diverse, with an abundance of tapas bars, restaurants, and markets serving up traditional Andalusian fare, such as gazpacho, paella, and Spanish omelette.

4. Natural Beauty:

Nestled at the foothills of the Sierra Nevada mountains, Granada is surrounded by breathtaking natural scenery.
Outdoor enthusiasts can explore the Sierra Nevada National Park, home to Spain's highest peak and a wealth of hiking trails, skiing slopes, and wildlife.
The Alpujarras region, with its picturesque villages, terraced hillsides, and thermal baths, offers a peaceful retreat from the hustle and bustle of city life.

5. Festivals and Events:

Throughout the year, Granada hosts a variety of cultural festivals and events that showcase the city's rich heritage and traditions.

The International Festival of Music and Dance, held in the Alhambra and other historic venues, features performances by world-renowned artists and musicians.

Other notable events include the Festival of Corpus Christi, Semana Santa (Holy Week), and the Granada International Jazz Festival, attracting visitors from around the globe.

6. Hospitality and Warmth:

Granada is renowned for its hospitality and warmth, with locals known for their friendliness and generosity towards visitors.

Whether exploring the city's historic landmarks, sampling local delicacies, or engaging in cultural activities, visitors to Granada are sure to feel welcomed and embraced by its vibrant community.

In conclusion, Granada offers a captivating blend of history, culture, and natural beauty that appeals to travelers of all interests and preferences. Whether exploring ancient palaces, savoring tapas in bustling plazas, or hiking in the mountains, a visit to Granada promises an unforgettable experience filled with discovery and wonder.

2.0 Planning Your Trip

2.1 Best Time to Visit

Choosing the right time to visit Granada depends on your preferences, as each season offers unique experiences and attractions. Here's an extensive overview of the best times to visit Granada:

1. Spring (March to May):

Spring is one of the most popular times to visit Granada, as the weather is mild and comfortable, with temperatures ranging from 15°C to 25°C (59°F to 77°F).

The city comes alive with vibrant colors as flowers bloom in gardens and parks, creating a picturesque backdrop for sightseeing and outdoor activities.

Visitors can enjoy exploring the Alhambra Palace and Generalife Gardens without the intense heat of summer, as well as attending cultural events and festivals held throughout the season.

2. Summer (June to August):

Summer is peak tourist season in Granada, with long days of sunshine and temperatures often exceeding 30°C (86°F), especially in July and August.

Despite the heat, summer attracts visitors eager to experience Granada's vibrant atmosphere, outdoor cafes, and lively nightlife.

It's important to stay hydrated and seek shade during the hottest hours of the day, but summer also offers the opportunity to cool off in the Sierra Nevada mountains or relax by the beach on day trips to the Costa del Sol.

3. Fall (September to November):

Fall is a delightful time to visit Granada, as temperatures begin to cool down, ranging from 15°C to 25°C (59°F to 77°F), and crowds start to thin out after the peak summer season.

The autumn foliage adds a splash of color to the city's landscapes, making it an ideal time for hiking in the Sierra Nevada or exploring the Alhambra and Albayzín district.

Fall also marks the harvest season, with local markets brimming with fresh fruits, vegetables, and artisanal products, offering visitors a taste of authentic Andalusian cuisine.

4. Winter (December to February):

Winter in Granada is mild compared to other parts of Europe, with daytime temperatures averaging around 10°C to 15°C (50°F to 59°F), although nights can be chilly.

While snowfall is not uncommon in the Sierra Nevada mountains, it rarely affects the city itself, making it an ideal time for winter sports enthusiasts to hit the slopes.

Winter also offers the opportunity to experience Granada's cultural attractions without the crowds, as well as festive events such as Christmas markets and New Year's celebrations.

5. Shoulder Seasons (March to May and September to November):

The shoulder seasons of spring and fall are considered some of the best times to visit Granada, as they offer a balance of pleasant weather, fewer crowds, and lower prices on accommodations and attractions. Visitors can take advantage of the mild temperatures to explore the city's historic landmarks, enjoy outdoor activities, and immerse themselves in the local culture without feeling overwhelmed by tourist crowds.

In summary, the best time to visit Granada depends on your preferences for weather, crowds, and activities. Whether you prefer the vibrant atmosphere of summer, the mild temperatures of spring and fall, or the festive ambiance of winter, Granada offers something for every traveler throughout the year.

2.2 Visa and Entry Requirements

1. Visa Exemption for EU/EEA/Swiss Citizens:

Citizens of the European Union (EU), European Economic Area (EEA), and Switzerland do not need a visa to enter Spain or Granada for stays of up to 90 days within a 180-day period.
They only need a valid passport or national ID card for entry and stay purposes.

2. Schengen Visa for Non-EU/EEA Citizens:

Citizens of countries not part of the EU, EEA, or Switzerland may need a Schengen visa to enter Spain, including Granada, for short stays.

The Schengen visa allows travelers to visit any of the 26 Schengen Area countries, including Spain, for tourism, business, or family visits.

Applicants must apply for a Schengen visa at the Spanish consulate or embassy in their home country before traveling to Spain.

3. Visa Waiver for Certain Countries:

Some non-EU/EEA countries have agreements with Spain that allow their citizens to enter for short stays without a visa.

These agreements typically apply to countries in Latin America, the Caribbean, and other regions with historical ties to Spain.

Travelers should check with the nearest Spanish consulate or embassy to determine if they are eligible for visa waiver and the specific requirements.

4. Long-Term Visa and Residence Permit:

Non-EU/EEA citizens planning to stay in Granada for longer than 90 days, such as for work, study, or family reunification, may need to apply for a long-term visa and residence permit.

The application process for a long-term visa and residence permit is more complex and may require additional documentation, such as proof of financial means, medical insurance, and a clean criminal record.

Applicants should start the application process well in advance of their intended arrival in Granada, as processing times can be lengthy.

5. Required Documents for Visa Application:

Passport: Must be valid for at least three months beyond the intended date of departure from Spain.

Visa application form: Completed and signed.

Passport-sized photos: Usually two recent photos meeting specific size and format requirements.

Travel itinerary: Including flight reservations, accommodation bookings, and details of planned activities in Granada.

Proof of financial means: Such as bank statements, traveler's checks, or sponsorship letters, to demonstrate the ability to cover expenses during the stay.

Travel insurance: Valid for the duration of the trip and providing coverage for medical emergencies, repatriation, and other unforeseen circumstances.

Additional documents may be required depending on the purpose of the visit, such as a letter of invitation, proof of enrollment in a Spanish educational institution, or a job contract from a Spanish employer.

6. Entry Requirements During COVID-19 Pandemic:

Travelers should check the latest travel advisories and entry requirements for Spain and Granada, including any COVID-19-related restrictions or quarantine measures.
Proof of vaccination, negative COVID-19 test results, or health declarations may be required for entry, depending on the current regulations in place.

7. Important Considerations:

Visa and entry requirements may vary depending on the traveler's nationality, purpose of visit, and length of stay.

It is essential to verify the specific requirements and application procedures applicable to your situation before traveling to Granada.

Travelers should allow sufficient time to complete the visa application process and ensure that all required documents are in order to avoid any delays or complications at the port of entry.

In summary, while citizens of EU/EEA countries enjoy visa-free travel to Granada for short stays, non-EU/EEA citizens may need to obtain a Schengen visa or other appropriate travel documents depending on their nationality and travel plans. Understanding and complying with the visa and entry requirements is crucial for a smooth and hassle-free visit to Granada, allowing travelers to focus on enjoying all that this beautiful city has to offer.

2.3 Currency and Banking

Granada, like the rest of Spain, operates on the Euro (€) as its official currency. Understanding the currency and banking system is essential for travelers visiting Granada. Here's an extensive overview:

1. Currency:

The Euro (€) is the official currency of Spain, including Granada. It is abbreviated as EUR.

The Euro is divided into 100 cents, with coins available in denominations of 1, 2, 5, 10, 20, and 50 cents, as well as 1 and 2 Euro coins.

Banknotes come in denominations of 5, 10, 20, 50, 100, 200, and 500 Euros.

The Euro is widely accepted throughout Granada for transactions, including shopping, dining, and accommodation.

2. Banking System:

Spain has a well-developed banking system, with numerous banks and financial institutions operating in Granada.

Some of the major banks in Spain include Banco Santander, BBVA, CaixaBank, Banco Sabadell, and Bankia.

Banking hours in Granada typically follow standard business hours, with most banks open from Monday to Friday, usually from 9:00 AM to 2:00 PM.

Some banks may also offer limited hours on Saturdays, and certain branches located in commercial areas or tourist areas may have extended hours.

3. ATMs:

ATMs (Automated Teller Machines) are widely available throughout Granada, offering convenient access to cash for both locals and travelers.
ATMs accept major international credit and debit cards, including Visa, Mastercard, American Express, and Maestro.

Travelers can withdraw Euros from ATMs using their debit or credit cards, although they may incur foreign transaction fees or currency conversion fees imposed by their home banks.

4. Currency Exchange:

Currency exchange services are available in Granada, primarily at banks, exchange offices (casas de cambio), and some hotels. Exchange rates may vary between providers, and it's advisable to compare rates and fees before exchanging currency.

Major currencies such as US Dollars, British Pounds, and Japanese Yen can typically be exchanged at most banks and exchange offices.

5. Credit and Debit Cards:

Credit and debit cards are widely accepted in Granada, especially in hotels, restaurants, shops, and tourist attractions.
Visa and Mastercard are the most commonly accepted card networks, followed

by American Express and Discover, although acceptance may vary.

It's recommended to inform your bank of your travel plans before departing for Granada to prevent any issues with card usage abroad.

6. Traveler's Checks:

Traveler's checks are less commonly used in Granada compared to credit/debit cards and cash.

While some banks may still accept traveler's checks, they are becoming increasingly obsolete, and travelers may encounter difficulty finding establishments willing to cash them.

7. Tips for Banking and Currency:

Carry a mix of cash and cards for payment convenience, as well as a backup source of funds in case of emergencies.

Notify your bank of your travel plans to avoid any unexpected card declines or security blocks while in Granada.

Keep track of exchange rates and fees to ensure you get the best value when exchanging currency or using cards abroad.

Be cautious when using ATMs, especially in tourist areas, and shield your PIN when entering it to prevent theft or fraud.

Understanding the currency and banking system in Granada ensures that travelers can manage their finances effectively and enjoy a seamless experience during their visit to this beautiful city in Spain.

2.4 Health and safety tips

Ensuring your health and safety during your visit to Granada is essential for a smooth and enjoyable experience. Here are extensive tips to help you stay healthy and safe while exploring this beautiful city:

1. Health Precautions:

Travel Insurance: Purchase comprehensive travel insurance before your trip to Granada to cover medical emergencies, trip cancellations, and other unforeseen events.

Medical Services: Familiarize yourself with the location of hospitals, clinics, and pharmacies in Granada, especially if you have any pre-existing medical conditions or require prescription medications.

Vaccinations: Ensure your routine vaccinations are up-to-date before traveling to Spain. Depending on your travel plans and medical history, you may also need additional vaccinations, so consult with your healthcare provider well in advance.

Sun Protection: Granada experiences long hours of sunshine, especially in the summer months. Protect yourself from sunburn and heatstroke by wearing sunscreen, sunglasses, and lightweight clothing, and staying hydrated throughout the day.

Water Safety: Tap water in Granada is generally safe to drink, but if you prefer, you can opt for bottled water, which is widely available at supermarkets and convenience stores.

2. Safety Tips:

Safety TIPS

Stay Informed: Stay updated on local news and advisories, especially regarding any safety concerns or emergency situations in Granada.

Crime Awareness: Granada is considered a safe city for travelers, but petty crimes such as pickpocketing and theft can occur, particularly in crowded tourist areas. Keep your belongings secure and be vigilant in crowded places, such as markets, public transportation, and tourist attractions.

Emergency Contacts: Familiarize yourself with emergency contact numbers, including the local police (Emergencias - 112), ambulance services, and your country's embassy or consulate in Spain.

Night Safety: Exercise caution when exploring Granada at night, especially if you are alone or in unfamiliar areas. Stick to well-lit and populated streets, and avoid isolated areas or walking alone in secluded alleys.

Traffic Safety: Be mindful of traffic when crossing streets in Granada, as drivers may not always yield to pedestrians. Use designated crosswalks, follow traffic signals, and look both ways before crossing.

Natural Hazards: While Granada is not prone to natural disasters, such as earthquakes or hurricanes, it's wise to be prepared for unexpected events. Familiarize yourself with evacuation procedures at your accommodation and have an emergency kit with essential supplies on hand.

3. COVID-19 Precautions:

Follow Guidelines: Adhere to local COVID-19 guidelines and regulations implemented by the Spanish government and health authorities. This may include wearing face masks in indoor public spaces, practicing physical distancing, and adhering to capacity limits in establishments.

Vaccination and Testing: Ensure you are fully vaccinated against COVID-19 before traveling to Granada. Depending on current regulations, you may also need to provide proof of a negative COVID-19 test result or undergo testing upon arrival.

Hygiene Practices: Practice good hygiene habits, such as frequent handwashing or using hand sanitizer, especially after touching surfaces in public areas.

By following these health and safety tips, you can enjoy a worry-free and memorable experience while exploring the captivating city of Granada. Remember to prioritize your well-being and take necessary precautions to safeguard your health and safety throughout your journey.

2.5 Packing Essentials

Packing effectively for your trip to Granada is essential to ensure you have everything you need for a comfortable and enjoyable stay. Here's an extensive list of packing essentials to consider:

1. Clothing:

Lightweight, breathable clothing suitable for warm weather, especially during the summer months when temperatures can soar.
Comfortable walking shoes for exploring Granada's cobblestone streets and historic sites.

Hat, sunglasses, and sunscreen to protect against the sun's rays.

Sweater or jacket for cooler evenings, especially in the spring and fall.

Swimwear if you plan to visit beaches or enjoy hotel pools.

Rain jacket or umbrella, as occasional showers can occur throughout the year.

2. Travel Accessories:

Passport, ID, and travel documents, including copies stored digitally or in a separate location.

Travel insurance information, including policy details and emergency contact numbers.

Money belt or secure wallet to keep valuables safe while exploring.

Electrical adapter and converter for charging electronic devices, as Spain uses the Europlug (Type C) and operates on 230V/50Hz electricity.

Portable power bank to keep your electronic devices charged while on the go.

Lightweight daypack or tote bag for carrying essentials during sightseeing excursions.

3. Toiletries and Personal Care:

Basic toiletries, including toothbrush, toothpaste, shampoo, conditioner, body wash, and moisturizer.

Prescription medications and any necessary medical supplies, along with copies of prescriptions.

First-aid kit with bandages, antiseptic wipes, pain relievers, and any other essential medications.

Insect repellent to protect against mosquitoes, especially during the warmer months.

Hand sanitizer or antibacterial wipes for maintaining hygiene while traveling.

4. Technology and Entertainment:

Smartphone or tablet with charger and travel apps for navigation, translation, and communication.

Camera or smartphone with camera for capturing memories of your trip.

E-reader or books for reading during downtime or while traveling.

Headphones or earbuds for listening to music,
podcasts, or audiobooks.

5. Miscellaneous Items:

Travel guidebook or maps of Granada to help navigate the city and plan activities.
Reusable water bottle to stay hydrated while exploring.
Snacks and energy bars for on-the-go nourishment during sightseeing excursions.
Travel-sized laundry detergent for washing clothes if needed.
Travel lock or luggage strap to secure your belongings while in transit or at your accommodation.

6. COVID-19 Essentials:

Face masks or coverings to comply with local regulations and protect yourself and others.

Hand sanitizer with at least 60% alcohol content for regular hand hygiene.

Disinfectant wipes for sanitizing surfaces, such as airplane seats or hotel room handles.

Personal protective equipment (PPE) as recommended by health authorities, such as gloves or face shields, if desired.

7. Optional Items:

Travel pillow and blanket for added comfort during long flights or train journeys.

Travel-sized umbrella or poncho for unexpected rain showers.

Travel journal or notebook for documenting your experiences and reflections during your trip.

Portable luggage scale to avoid overweight baggage fees when flying.

By packing these essentials for your trip to Granada, you'll be well-prepared to make the most of your time in this enchanting city. Remember to consider the season, activities planned, and personal preferences when selecting items to bring along, and aim for a balance between comfort, practicality, and convenience.

3.0 Transportation

3.1 Getting to Granada

Getting to Granada can be an exciting part of your travel experience, with various transportation options available to reach this enchanting city in southern Spain. Here's an extensive overview of the ways to get to Granada:

1. By Air:

Granada Airport (Federico García Lorca Granada-Jaén Airport - GRX):

Located approximately 15 kilometers west of Granada city center, Granada Airport offers domestic and international flights.

Domestic flights: Granada Airport serves as a hub for domestic flights within Spain, with connections to cities such as Madrid, Barcelona, Valencia, and Palma de Mallorca.

International flights: While fewer in number, Granada Airport also offers some international flights to destinations such as London, Paris, Milan, and Casablanca.

Malaga Airport (AGP): Alternatively, travelers can fly into Malaga Airport, which is approximately 130 kilometers south of Granada. Malaga Airport offers a wider range of domestic and international flights and is well-connected to Granada by road and public transportation.

2. By Train:

Renfe Train Services: Granada is connected to major cities in Spain by the national railway network operated by Renfe.
High-speed AVE trains: AVE trains provide fast and comfortable connections between

Granada and cities such as Madrid, Barcelona, Seville, and Valencia.

Regional trains: Regional trains also serve Granada, offering connections to nearby cities and towns within Andalusia and beyond.

Granada Train Station (Estación de Granada): The main train station in Granada is located in the northern part of the city center, providing easy access to local transportation and accommodation options.

3. By Bus:

Alsa Bus Services: Alsa operates long-distance bus services connecting Granada to cities and towns throughout Spain.

Buses from major cities: Alsa buses offer frequent connections to Granada from cities such as Madrid, Barcelona, Malaga, Seville, and Valencia.

Regional and local buses: Additionally, local and regional bus services provide connections to nearby towns and attractions within Andalusia.

Granada Bus Station (Estación de Autobuses de Granada): The main bus station in Granada is centrally located near the city center, offering convenient access to public transportation and nearby amenities.

4. By Car:

Driving from Major Cities: Granada is accessible by car from major cities in Spain via well-maintained highways and roads.

From Madrid: The journey from Madrid to Granada by car takes approximately 4-5 hours via the A-44 highway.

From Malaga: The drive from Malaga to Granada takes approximately 1.5-2 hours via the A-92 highway.

From Seville: Driving from Seville to Granada takes approximately 2.5-3 hours via the A-92 highway.

Rental Cars: Travelers can rent cars from various rental agencies at airports, train stations, and city centers in Granada and other major cities.

5. By Shared or Private Transfers:

Private Transfers: Private transfer services are available for travelers who prefer the convenience and comfort of door-to-door transportation. Companies offer private transfers from airports, train stations, or hotels to Granada and other destinations.

Shared Transfers: Shared shuttle services may also be available, offering a cost-effective option for travelers to share transportation with others heading to similar destinations.

6. Local Transportation in Granada:

Upon arrival in Granada, travelers can utilize local transportation options, including buses, taxis, and rental bikes, to explore the city and its surrounding areas.

By considering these various transportation options, travelers can choose the most convenient and suitable method to reach Granada and begin their unforgettable journey in this captivating city. It's advisable to plan and book transportation in advance, especially during peak travel seasons, to ensure a smooth and hassle-free journey to Granada.

3.2 Getting Around Granada

Navigating Granada and getting around the city is relatively straightforward, thanks to its well-developed public transportation system, walkable city center, and various transportation options. Here's an extensive overview of getting around Granada:

1. Public Transportation:

Bus Services: Granada has an extensive network of urban buses operated by the Transportes Rober company, providing convenient and affordable transportation around the city.

The bus network covers all major neighborhoods and attractions in Granada, including the Alhambra, Albayzín, Sacromonte, and the city center.

Bus tickets can be purchased on board from the driver or at designated ticket machines located at major bus stops.

Metro de Granada: The Granada Metro is a light rail system that connects various parts of the city, including the city center, Alhambra, and outer neighborhoods.

The metro operates on two lines: the Albolote-Granada line (Line 1) and the Armilla-Granada line (Line 2), providing efficient transportation for commuters and tourists alike.

Tickets for the metro can be purchased at stations using ticket machines or at select kiosks.

2. Walking:

Granada's city center is compact and pedestrian-friendly, making it easy to explore on foot.

Many of the city's attractions, such as the Alhambra, Cathedral, Royal Chapel, and Albayzín district, are within walking distance of each other.

Walking allows visitors to soak in the charming atmosphere of Granada's streets, discover hidden gems, and appreciate the city's architectural and cultural heritage.

3. Bicycles:

Granada offers bicycle rental services, allowing visitors to explore the city at their own pace while enjoying the flexibility and eco-friendly mode of transportation.
Several rental companies and bike shops in Granada offer a range of bicycles, including city bikes, mountain bikes, and electric

bikes, for rent by the hour, day, or longer periods.
Dedicated bike lanes and bike-friendly routes make cycling a convenient and enjoyable way to get around Granada and explore its surroundings.

4. Taxis and Ride-Sharing:

Taxis are readily available throughout Granada and can be hailed on the street or found at designated taxi stands.
Taxi services provide a convenient option for travelers to reach specific destinations or travel outside the city center, such as to the airport, bus station, or Alhambra.
Ride-sharing services such as Uber and Cabify are also available in Granada, offering an alternative to traditional taxis for getting around the city.

5. Car Rentals:

While Granada's city center is best explored on foot or using public transportation, renting a car can be advantageous for travelers who wish to explore the surrounding areas or embark on day trips to nearby attractions.

Several car rental companies operate in Granada, offering a range of vehicles to suit different budgets and preferences.

It's important to note that parking in Granada's city center can be limited and expensive, so travelers should consider parking options and fees when renting a car.

6. Hop-On Hop-Off Bus Tours:

Hop-on hop-off bus tours provide a convenient and flexible way for visitors to explore Granada's top attractions and landmarks.

These guided tours typically follow designated routes with stops at major points of interest, allowing passengers to disembark and explore at their own pace before hopping back on the next bus.

7. Accessibility:

Granada's public transportation system and many tourist attractions are accessible to travelers with mobility challenges, with provisions for wheelchair access, ramps, elevators, and other accommodations.

By utilizing these various transportation options, visitors can navigate Granada with ease and efficiency, allowing them to make the most of their time in this captivating city filled with history, culture, and architectural wonders.

3.3 Public Transportation

Public transportation in Granada plays a crucial role in facilitating travel within the city and its surrounding areas, offering residents and visitors convenient, efficient, and affordable mobility options. Here's an extensive overview of public transportation in Granada:

1. Bus Services:

Granada's urban bus network is operated by Transportes Rober, providing comprehensive coverage of the city and its outskirts.
The bus network comprises numerous routes serving neighborhoods, suburbs, and major attractions, including the Alhambra, Albayzín, Sacromonte, and city center.
Buses run frequently throughout the day, with extended service hours on weekdays

and weekends, making it convenient for passengers to travel around Granada at any time.

Tickets can be purchased on board from the driver or at ticket machines located at major bus stops. Additionally, multi-trip passes and tourist cards offering unlimited bus travel for a specified duration are available for purchase.

2. Metro de Granada:

The Granada Metro is a modern light rail system that complements the city's bus network, providing efficient transportation across different parts of Granada.

The metro currently operates two lines:

Line 1 (Albolote-Granada): Connects the northern suburbs of Granada, such as Albolote and Maracena, with the city center and other key destinations.

Line 2 (Armilla-Granada): Links the municipality of Armilla to the city center, passing through important areas like the University Campus and Health Sciences Campus.

The metro system features modern stations equipped with amenities such as ticket vending machines, electronic ticket validators, elevators, and accessibility features for passengers with reduced mobility.

3. Taxi Services:

Taxis are a convenient mode of transportation in Granada, offering door-to-door service for passengers who prefer a more direct and personalized travel experience.

Taxis can be hailed on the street, found at designated taxi stands throughout the city, or booked in advance via phone or mobile app.

Taxi fares are regulated by the local government and typically consist of a base fare plus additional charges based on distance traveled and time spent in traffic.

4. Bicycle Rentals:

Granada promotes cycling as an eco-friendly and healthy transportation option, with dedicated bike lanes and bike-friendly routes throughout the city.

Several bike rental companies and shops in Granada offer a range of bicycles for rent, including city bikes, mountain bikes, electric bikes, and tandem bikes.

Cyclists can explore Granada at their own pace, enjoying the freedom and flexibility to discover the city's attractions, parks, and scenic pathways.

5. Accessibility:

Granada's public transportation system is designed to be accessible to passengers with disabilities and reduced mobility, with features such as low-floor buses, wheelchair ramps, priority seating, and audible announcements.
Metro stations, bus stops, and vehicles are equipped with facilities to accommodate passengers with special needs, ensuring inclusivity and equal access to transportation services.

6. Integration and Connectivity:

Granada's public transportation services are integrated to provide seamless connectivity between different modes of transportation, allowing passengers to transfer easily between buses, metro lines, and other transportation options.

Integrated ticketing systems and multi-modal passes enable passengers to use multiple modes of transportation within a single journey, streamlining the travel experience and promoting sustainable mobility.

Overall, public transportation in Granada offers a reliable, accessible, and environmentally friendly means of travel for residents and visitors alike, contributing to the city's sustainability, accessibility, and quality of life.

4.0 Accommodation

4.1 Luxury hotel

Granada, with its rich history, stunning architecture, and vibrant culture, offers a range of luxury accommodations that cater to discerning travelers seeking comfort, elegance, and exceptional service. Here's an extensive guide to luxury hotels in Granada:

1. Alhambra Palace Hotel:

Situated just steps away from the iconic Alhambra Palace, this historic hotel exudes charm and sophistication.

The Alhambra Palace Hotel boasts luxurious rooms and suites with breathtaking views of the Alhambra, the Generalife gardens, and the city of Granada.

Guests can indulge in fine dining at the hotel's renowned restaurant, which serves exquisite Spanish and international cuisine, accompanied by panoramic views of Granada.

Other amenities include a spa and wellness center, outdoor swimming pool, elegant lounges, and event spaces for weddings, conferences, and special occasions.

2. Hospes Palacio de los Patos:

Housed in a beautifully restored 19th-century palace, Hospes Palacio de los Patos offers a blend of historic charm and contemporary luxury.

The hotel features elegant rooms and suites with stylish décor, modern amenities, and plush furnishings, creating a serene retreat for guests.

Guests can unwind and rejuvenate at the hotel's wellness center, which includes a spa, sauna, steam room, and fitness facilities.

The hotel's restaurant offers innovative cuisine inspired by Andalusian flavors, complemented by a selection of fine wines and cocktails.

With its tranquil garden, courtyard, and terrace, Hospes Palacio de los Patos provides a peaceful oasis in the heart of Granada.

3. AC Palacio de Santa Paula, Autograph Collection:

Set within a former convent dating back to the 16th century, AC Palacio de Santa

Paula offers a luxurious retreat in the historic center of Granada.

The hotel features elegantly appointed rooms and suites, blending historic architecture with modern comforts and amenities.

Guests can savor gourmet cuisine at the hotel's restaurant, which showcases traditional Andalusian dishes with a contemporary twist.

The hotel's wellness center includes a spa, fitness center, and sauna, providing guests with opportunities for relaxation and rejuvenation.

With its central location near Granada's main attractions, including the Cathedral and Royal Chapel, AC Palacio de Santa Paula offers a convenient base for exploring the city.

4. Barceló Carmen Granada:

Located in the heart of Granada, near the vibrant shopping and dining district of Calle Navas, Barceló Carmen Granada offers modern luxury and convenience.

The hotel features spacious rooms and suites with contemporary décor, comfortable furnishings, and views of the city or Sierra Nevada mountains.

Guests can enjoy a range of amenities, including a rooftop terrace with panoramic views, outdoor swimming pool, fitness center, and spa.

The hotel's restaurant serves a variety of Mediterranean and international dishes, as well as tapas and cocktails in a stylish setting.

With its central location and upscale amenities, Barceló Carmen Granada provides a perfect blend of comfort, convenience, and luxury for travelers visiting Granada.

5. Eurostars Gran Vía Hotel:

Situated in a historic building on Granada's main thoroughfare, Eurostars Gran Vía Hotel offers elegant accommodations and modern amenities.

The hotel features spacious rooms and suites with contemporary design, luxurious bedding, and state-of-the-art technology.

Guests can relax and unwind at the hotel's rooftop terrace, which offers stunning views of Granada's skyline and the Sierra Nevada mountains.

The hotel's restaurant serves a variety of gourmet dishes inspired by local and international cuisine, accompanied by an extensive wine list.

With its prime location and upscale facilities, Eurostars Gran Vía Hotel provides a luxurious and convenient base for exploring Granada's attractions and landmarks.

These luxury hotels in Granada offer a combination of exquisite accommodations, exceptional service, and prime locations, providing travelers with an unforgettable experience in this captivating city. Whether you're visiting for leisure or business, these hotels promise indulgence, relaxation, and sophistication amidst the beauty and history of Granada.

4.2 Budget-Friendly Options

Granada, known for its rich history, stunning architecture, and vibrant culture, offers a variety of budget-friendly accommodation options for travelers seeking affordable yet comfortable places to stay. Here's an extensive guide to budget-friendly options in Granada:

1. Hostels:

Granada is home to numerous hostels catering to budget-conscious travelers, offering dormitory-style rooms, private rooms, and shared facilities such as kitchens, common areas, and social activities.

Hostels provide an affordable accommodation option with rates typically lower than traditional hotels, making them ideal for solo travelers, backpackers, and budget-minded groups.

Many hostels in Granada are centrally located, allowing guests to explore the city's attractions, nightlife, and dining options on foot.

2. Guesthouses and Pensiones:

Guesthouses and pensiones are budget-friendly accommodations offering private rooms with basic amenities, often at lower rates than hotels.

These family-run establishments provide a cozy and intimate atmosphere, with personalized service and local hospitality.

While guesthouses and pensiones may not offer the same level of luxury as upscale hotels, they provide comfortable and affordable lodging options for travelers seeking value and authenticity.

3. Budget Hotels:

Granada boasts a range of budget hotels that provide affordable accommodations without compromising on comfort or convenience.

Budget hotels in Granada typically offer clean and comfortable rooms with essential amenities such as Wi-Fi, air conditioning, and private bathrooms.

These hotels may not have extensive facilities or luxurious décor, but they provide a practical and economical option for travelers looking to save on accommodation costs.

4. Apartment Rentals:

Renting an apartment or vacation rental can be a cost-effective option for budget-conscious travelers, especially for families, groups, or those planning an extended stay in Granada.
Apartment rentals offer the flexibility of self-catering, allowing guests to prepare meals and snacks in a fully equipped kitchen, thus saving on dining expenses.
Many apartment rentals in Granada are located in residential neighborhoods, providing a more authentic and immersive experience of local life.

5. Camping and Hostels Rurales:

For outdoor enthusiasts and nature lovers, camping and rural hostels (hostels rurales) offer budget-friendly accommodation options in the countryside surrounding Granada.
Camping facilities range from campgrounds with basic amenities to eco-friendly glamping sites with comfortable tents and facilities.
Rural hostels provide rustic yet charming accommodations in rural settings, allowing guests to enjoy nature, outdoor activities, and relaxation away from the city.

6. Booking Tips for Budget-Friendly Accommodations:

Plan and book accommodation in advance to secure the best rates, especially during peak travel seasons and popular festivals.

Consider staying outside the city center to find more affordable accommodation options, with easy access to public transportation for exploring Granada's attractions.

Look for special offers, discounts, and promotional deals offered by hotels, hostels, and vacation rental platforms to maximize savings on accommodation costs.

Check traveler reviews and ratings on reputable booking websites to ensure that budget-friendly accommodations meet your expectations in terms of cleanliness, comfort, and location.

By choosing budget-friendly accommodation options in Granada, travelers can experience all that this captivating city has to offer without breaking the bank. Whether you're exploring historic landmarks, enjoying tapas in local taverns, or immersing yourself in Andalusian culture, affordable lodging options provide a comfortable and convenient base for your adventures in Granada.

4.3 Boutique Hotels

Granada, with its rich history, cultural heritage, and stunning architecture, offers a selection of boutique hotels that provide travelers with a unique and memorable lodging experience. Boutique hotels in Granada are characterized by their intimate atmosphere, personalized service, and attention to detail, offering guests a blend of charm, elegance, and comfort. Here's an extensive guide to boutique hotels in Granada:

1. Palacio de Santa Inés:

Housed in a beautifully restored 16th-century palace in the heart of Granada's historic Albaicín district, Palacio de Santa Inés exudes charm and character. The hotel features individually decorated rooms and suites, each showcasing original architectural details, antique furnishings, and modern amenities.

Guests can relax in the hotel's tranquil courtyard garden, enjoy panoramic views of the Alhambra from the rooftop terrace, or unwind in the cozy lounge with a selection of books and board games.

With its prime location near the Alhambra, Cathedral, and other major attractions, Palacio de Santa Inés offers a convenient and romantic retreat for couples and travelers seeking an authentic Granada experience.

2. Casa 1800 Granada:

Nestled in the heart of Granada's historic center, Casa 1800 Granada occupies a beautifully restored 17th-century mansion, blending period charm with modern comforts.

The hotel's elegant rooms and suites feature stylish décor, luxurious bedding, and amenities such as flat-screen TVs, minibars, and complimentary Wi-Fi.

Guests can enjoy complimentary afternoon tea in the hotel's charming courtyard or unwind in the rooftop terrace with panoramic views of the city and the Alhambra.

Casa 1800 Granada offers a tranquil and romantic setting, perfect for couples seeking a romantic getaway or honeymoon in Granada.

3. El Ladron de Agua:

Located just steps away from the Alhambra, El Ladron de Agua is a boutique hotel housed in a beautifully restored 16th-century palace overlooking the Darro River.

The hotel's rooms and suites feature elegant décor, handcrafted furnishings, and modern amenities, creating a luxurious and comfortable retreat for guests.

Guests can enjoy complimentary breakfast served in the hotel's cozy dining room or on

the rooftop terrace with stunning views of the Alhambra and the Albayzín district.
With its prime location and intimate ambiance, El Ladron de Agua offers a tranquil oasis in the heart of Granada, ideal for couples, honeymooners, and travelers seeking romance and relaxation.

4. Gar Anat Hotel Boutique:

Set in a historic building dating back to the 17th century, Gar Anat Hotel Boutique combines historic charm with contemporary style, offering a unique and memorable stay in Granada.

The hotel's rooms and suites are elegantly appointed, featuring modern amenities, luxurious bedding, and views of the city or the hotel's courtyard.

Guests can relax in the hotel's cozy lounge with a fireplace, enjoy a drink at the bar, or explore the nearby attractions, including the Cathedral, Royal Chapel, and Alcaicería market.

Gar Anat Hotel Boutique provides a boutique hotel experience characterized by its warm hospitality, attention to detail, and personalized service.

5. Casa Morisca:

Tucked away in the historic Albayzín district, Casa Morisca is a boutique hotel housed in a beautifully restored Moorish palace dating back to the 15th century.

The hotel's rooms and suites feature traditional Moorish architecture, with intricate tilework, arched doorways, and hand-carved wooden ceilings, creating a romantic and atmospheric setting.

Guests can relax in the hotel's courtyard garden, enjoy panoramic views of the Alhambra from the rooftop terrace, or indulge in traditional Andalusian cuisine at the hotel's restaurant.

Casa Morisca offers a unique and enchanting retreat for travelers seeking an authentic Granada experience immersed in history, culture, and romance.

These boutique hotels in Granada offer a unique and intimate lodging experience, combining historic charm, elegant design, and personalized service to create a memorable stay for guests. Whether you're exploring the city's historic landmarks, savoring Andalusian cuisine, or simply relaxing in the hotel's tranquil surroundings, boutique hotels in Granada provide a memorable and enchanting escape in one of Spain's most captivating cities.

4.4 Airbnb and Vacation Rentals

Granada, with its captivating blend of history, culture, and natural beauty, offers travelers a range of accommodation options beyond traditional hotels and hostels. Airbnb and vacation rentals provide visitors with the opportunity to immerse themselves in the local culture, enjoy unique accommodations, and experience Granada like a local. Here's an extensive overview of Airbnb and vacation rentals in Granada:

1. Variety of Options:

Airbnb and vacation rentals in Granada come in a variety of options, including apartments, condos, houses, villas, and even unique properties such as caves, palaces, and historic residences.
These accommodations cater to travelers of all preferences and group sizes, from solo

travelers and couples to families and large groups, offering flexibility and customization in terms of space, amenities, and location.

2. Authentic Local Experience:

Staying in an Airbnb or vacation rental allows travelers to experience Granada like a local, immersing themselves in residential neighborhoods, interacting with neighbors, and exploring hidden gems off the beaten path.
Hosts often provide insider tips and recommendations on local attractions, dining spots, and cultural experiences, enhancing the authenticity of the travel experience and providing valuable insights into Granada's culture and lifestyle.

3. Home-like Comfort and Amenities:

Airbnb and vacation rentals offer the comfort and convenience of a home away from home, with amenities such as fully equipped kitchens, living areas, bedrooms, bathrooms, and laundry facilities.

Guests can enjoy the flexibility of preparing their own meals, relaxing in spacious living areas, and unwinding in private bedrooms, creating a comfortable and personalized lodging experience.

4. Cost-Effective Option:

Airbnb and vacation rentals often provide better value for money compared to traditional hotels, especially for groups or families traveling together.

Guests can benefit from lower nightly rates, especially for longer stays, as well as cost savings on dining expenses by preparing meals in the rental's kitchen.

5. Privacy and Independence:

Airbnb and vacation rentals offer privacy and independence, allowing guests to come and go as they please, without the restrictions of hotel check-in/check-out times or housekeeping schedules.
Guests have exclusive use of the rental property, giving them the freedom to relax, socialize, and enjoy their vacation at their own pace.

6. Personalized Service and Communication:

Many Airbnb hosts and vacation rental managers offer personalized service and communication, providing guests with assistance, recommendations, and support throughout their stay.
Hosts may greet guests upon arrival, offer local tips and insights, and be available to

address any questions or concerns during the guest's stay, enhancing the overall experience and satisfaction.

7. Safety and Trust:

Airbnb and vacation rental platforms prioritize safety and trust, with features such as verified listings, secure payment systems, and guest reviews to help travelers make informed decisions and feel confident about their choice of accommodation.
Hosts are required to meet certain standards and guidelines set by the platform, ensuring a level of quality and reliability for guests.

8. Sustainability and Eco-Friendliness:

Some Airbnb hosts and vacation rental properties in Granada emphasize sustainability and eco-friendliness, implementing practices such as energy conservation, waste reduction, and eco-friendly amenities to minimize environmental impact.

In summary, Airbnb and vacation rentals in Granada offer travelers a flexible, personalized, and immersive lodging experience, allowing them to enjoy the comforts of home while exploring this enchanting city. Whether you're seeking a cozy apartment in the city center, a charming villa in the countryside, or a unique property with historical significance, Airbnb and vacation rentals provide a wide range of options to suit every traveler's preferences and budget.

5.0 Shopping Guide

5.1 Shopping mall

Granada, known for its rich history, stunning architecture, and vibrant culture, is also home to several modern shopping malls that offer a diverse array of retail, dining, entertainment, and leisure options. From international brands to local boutiques, these shopping centers provide visitors and residents with a convenient and enjoyable shopping experience. Here's an extensive overview of shopping malls in Granada:

1. Nevada Shopping:

Located on the outskirts of Granada, Nevada Shopping is the largest shopping mall in the province of Granada and one of the largest in Andalusia.

The mall boasts over 180 stores, including international fashion brands, electronics retailers, department stores, home furnishings, and specialty shops.

Nevada Shopping also features a wide range of dining options, from fast-food chains to sit-down restaurants serving Spanish and international cuisine.

In addition to shopping and dining, the mall offers entertainment and leisure facilities such as a multiplex cinema, bowling alley, children's play area, and fitness center.

Nevada Shopping provides ample parking space, easy access via public transportation, and amenities such as free Wi-Fi and baby changing facilities, ensuring a convenient and enjoyable shopping experience for visitors of all ages.

2. Centro Comercial Serrallo Plaza:

Situated in the southern part of Granada, Centro Comercial Serrallo Plaza is a popular shopping and entertainment destination for locals and tourists alike.

The mall features a diverse mix of retail stores, including fashion boutiques, beauty salons, bookshops, and specialty shops selling jewelry, accessories, and gifts.

Serrallo Plaza offers a wide range of dining options, from casual eateries and coffee shops to upscale restaurants serving Mediterranean and international cuisine.

Visitors can enjoy leisure and entertainment activities such as a multiscreen cinema, indoor playground, trampoline park, and arcade games.

With its family-friendly atmosphere, outdoor seating areas, and regular events and promotions, Centro Comercial Serrallo Plaza provides a lively and dynamic shopping experience in Granada.

3. Centro Comercial Neptuno:

Located in the heart of Granada, Centro Comercial Neptuno is a modern shopping center with a convenient location near the city's main attractions, hotels, and transportation hubs.

The mall features a diverse selection of shops, including fashion retailers, shoe stores, electronics outlets, and supermarkets, catering to a wide range of tastes and budgets.

Neptuno offers a variety of dining options, from fast-food chains and cafes to international restaurants and tapas bars, serving local specialties and global cuisine.

Visitors can take advantage of additional services and amenities at Neptuno, such as ATMs, pharmacies, beauty salons, and a post office, making it a one-stop destination for shopping and errands.

With its central location, modern facilities, and ample parking, Centro Comercial

Neptuno provides a convenient and enjoyable shopping experience for residents and visitors alike.

4. Granaita Shopping Center:

Situated in the northern part of Granada, Granaita Shopping Center is a relatively new addition to the city's retail landscape, offering a diverse mix of stores and services.
The mall features well-known fashion brands, sports retailers, home décor stores, and specialty shops selling cosmetics, accessories, and gifts.
Granaita Shopping Center also houses a variety of dining options, including fast-food outlets, cafes, and restaurants serving international cuisine and local delicacies.

Visitors can enjoy leisure activities such as a multiscreen cinema, video game arcade, and children's entertainment area, providing fun and entertainment for the whole family.

With its modern design, spacious layout, and convenient location near major roadways, Granaita Shopping Center offers a contemporary and accessible shopping experience in Granada.

5. Megacentro:

Situated in the northern part of Granada, Megacentro is a large shopping complex that caters to a diverse range of retail, dining, and leisure needs.

The mall features a mix of national and international brands, including fashion retailers, electronics stores, home goods outlets, and specialty shops.

Megacentro offers a variety of dining options, from fast-food chains and casual eateries to upscale restaurants and cafes serving Spanish and international cuisine.

Visitors can enjoy entertainment and leisure activities such as a multiplex cinema, bowling alley, indoor playground, and fitness center, providing entertainment for all ages.

With its spacious parking facilities, accessibility via public transportation, and amenities such as free Wi-Fi and baby changing facilities, Megacentro provides a convenient and enjoyable shopping experience for residents and visitors alike.

6. Accessibility and Amenities:

Shopping malls in Granada are easily accessible by car, public transportation, and pedestrian walkways, with ample parking facilities, taxi stands, and bus stops nearby. Many malls offer additional amenities and services to enhance the shopping experience, such as free Wi-Fi, baby changing facilities, ATMs, pharmacies, and customer service desks.

Visitors can take advantage of special promotions, discounts, and events offered by malls throughout the year, including seasonal sales, holiday festivities, and cultural celebrations.

In summary, shopping malls in Granada offer a diverse and dynamic retail environment, catering to a wide range of tastes, preferences, and budgets. Whether you're looking for fashion, electronics, home goods, or dining options, these modern shopping centers provide a convenient and enjoyable destination for residents and visitors to shop, dine, and socialize in the heart of Andalusia.

5.2 Local Markets

Granada's local markets are vibrant hubs of activity where visitors can immerse themselves in the city's rich cultural heritage, sample delicious regional specialties, and discover an array of fresh produce, artisanal crafts, and unique souvenirs. From traditional markets selling fresh fruits and vegetables to bustling flea markets offering antiques and vintage finds, Granada's markets offer a sensory feast for travelers of all interests. Here's an extensive guide to exploring the local markets in Granada:

1. Mercado de San Agustín:

Located in the heart of Granada's historic center, Mercado de San Agustín is one of the city's oldest and most beloved markets.

The market features a wide selection of stalls selling fresh fruits, vegetables, meats, seafood, cheeses, olives, spices, and other culinary delights sourced from local producers.

Visitors can sample traditional Andalusian specialties such as jamón ibérico, Manchego cheese, marinated olives, and freshly baked bread, as well as international delicacies from around the world.

In addition to food vendors, Mercado de San Agustín also hosts artisanal craftsmen selling handmade ceramics, jewelry, textiles, leather goods, and other unique products.

2. Mercado Central de Abastos:

Located near Granada's train station, Mercado Central de Abastos is a bustling wholesale market where locals and chefs come to purchase fresh ingredients for their kitchens.

The market offers a wide range of products, including fruits, vegetables, meats, fish, spices, dried goods, and specialty items such as local cheeses, cured meats, and Andalusian wines.

Visitors can explore the colorful stalls, interact with vendors, and experience the lively atmosphere of this traditional market, which has been serving the community for over a century.

Mercado Central de Abastos also hosts occasional events, such as cooking demonstrations, food tastings, and cultural performances, adding to the vibrancy and excitement of the market.

3. Alcaicería:

Located in the heart of Granada's historic Albaicín district, Alcaicería is a labyrinthine maze of narrow streets and alleys lined with shops selling traditional Moorish crafts, textiles, ceramics, and souvenirs.

Historically, Alcaicería was a bustling silk market during the Moorish period, and today it continues to be a vibrant center of commerce and culture.
Visitors can browse a wide array of products, including hand-painted ceramics, intricately woven textiles, ornate lamps, colorful rugs, and intricately carved woodwork, all crafted by local artisans.

Alcaicería also offers a variety of culinary delights, including spices, teas, dried fruits, nuts, and sweets, providing a sensory experience that transports visitors back in time to Granada's Moorish past.

4. Flea Markets:

Granada is home to several flea markets where visitors can hunt for bargains, vintage treasures, and unique finds.
The Rastro de Granada, held every Sunday in the Plaza de Toros, is one of the city's largest flea markets, featuring a wide range of goods, including antiques, collectibles, clothing, accessories, books, and artwork.
Other flea markets in Granada include the Mercadillo del Zaidín, Mercadillo del Almanjayar, and Mercadillo de La Chana, each offering its own unique selection of items and a lively atmosphere.

5. Tips for Exploring Local Markets:

Arrive early in the morning to experience the markets at their liveliest, with vendors setting up their stalls and locals shopping for fresh produce.

Bring cash, as many vendors may not accept credit cards, especially at smaller markets and flea markets.

Don't be afraid to haggle, especially at flea markets and artisan stalls, where bargaining is a common practice.
Take your time to wander through the markets, soak in the sights, sounds, and smells, and interact with vendors to learn more about their products and traditions.

6. Sustainability and Eco-Friendliness:

Many local markets in Granada emphasize sustainability and eco-friendliness, with vendors offering organic, locally sourced, and environmentally friendly products.
Visitors can support small-scale producers, reduce their carbon footprint, and enjoy fresher, healthier foods by shopping at local markets instead of supermarkets.

In summary, Granada's local markets offer travelers a unique opportunity to experience the city's vibrant culture, culinary traditions, and artisanal craftsmanship. Whether you're browsing for fresh produce, hunting for vintage treasures, or simply soaking in the lively atmosphere, exploring the local markets is a must-do activity for visitors to Granada.

5.3 Unique Souvenirs

Granada, with its rich history, stunning architecture, and vibrant culture, offers a plethora of unique souvenirs that capture the essence of this enchanting city. From traditional crafts and artisanal products to culinary delights and cultural treasures,

Granada's souvenirs provide travelers with tangible memories of their journey and make thoughtful gifts for loved ones. Here's an extensive guide to some of the most distinctive souvenirs you can find in Granada:

1. Moorish-Inspired Crafts:

Granada's Moorish heritage is reflected in its artisanal crafts, including intricate ceramics, colorful tiles, and ornate lamps adorned with geometric patterns and Arabic motifs.

Visitors can purchase hand-painted ceramic tiles, pottery, and tableware featuring traditional Andalusian designs, as well as decorative tiles and plaques inspired by the Alhambra's stunning architecture.

Other Moorish-inspired crafts include intricately carved wooden boxes, mirrors, and furniture, as well as brass lanterns and tea sets reminiscent of the Alcaicería's bustling bazaars.

2. Handwoven Textiles:

Granada is renowned for its handwoven textiles, including colorful rugs, tapestries, and shawls crafted using traditional techniques passed down through generations.

Visitors can find a variety of textiles made from natural fibers such as wool, cotton, and silk, featuring intricate patterns, vibrant colors, and exquisite craftsmanship.

Local artisans also produce embroidered linens, cushion covers, and wall hangings inspired by Andalusian culture and nature, making them unique and meaningful souvenirs to cherish.

3. Andalusian Ceramics:

Granada's ceramic tradition dates back centuries, with local artisans producing a wide range of pottery, tiles, and decorative objects that showcase the region's cultural heritage.

Visitors can explore workshops and studios in Granada's Albaicín and Sacromonte neighborhoods to discover handcrafted ceramics, including decorative plates, vases, and tiles adorned with traditional motifs and vibrant glazes.

Many ceramic pieces feature intricate arabesque patterns, floral motifs, and calligraphic designs inspired by the Alhambra's exquisite tilework, adding a touch of Andalusian elegance to any home.

4. Local Delicacies:

No visit to Granada is complete without sampling its culinary delights, which make for delicious souvenirs to bring home or share with friends and family.

Visitors can purchase locally produced olive oil, wine, and cheese, as well as cured meats such as jamón ibérico and chorizo, which are renowned for their quality and flavor.

Other popular food souvenirs from Granada include artisanal chocolates, pastries, and sweets, such as piononos (a traditional dessert made with sponge cake and cream) and alfajores (almond cookies filled with dulce de leche), which showcase the region's sweet tooth and culinary creativity.

5. Flamenco Memorabilia:

Flamenco, the passionate and expressive dance form originating from Andalusia, holds a special place in Granada's cultural heritage, and visitors can find a variety of flamenco-related souvenirs to commemorate their visit.

Souvenirs include flamenco fans, castanets, shawls, and accessories adorned with flamenco motifs, as well as CDs, DVDs, and books featuring flamenco music, dance, and history.

For a truly unique souvenir, visitors can attend a flamenco show in Granada and purchase a handmade flamenco dress or costume from local artisans, providing an authentic memento of their flamenco experience.

6. Traditional Instruments:

Granada is famous for its musical traditions, and visitors can find a variety of traditional instruments and musical souvenirs to bring home.

Flamenco guitars, handcrafted by local luthiers using traditional methods and materials, are sought-after souvenirs for music lovers and collectors alike.

Other musical souvenirs include Spanish guitars, ukuleles, and percussion instruments such as cajónes (box drums) and tambourines, which capture the rhythm and spirit of Andalusian music.

7. Islamic Calligraphy and Art:

Granada's Islamic heritage is evident in its exquisite calligraphy and art, which can be found in the city's mosques, palaces, and historic monuments.

Visitors can purchase calligraphic artwork, manuscripts, and prints featuring verses from the Quran, poetry, and traditional Arabic sayings, as well as intricate arabesque designs and geometric patterns.

Other Islamic-inspired souvenirs include ornamental brass lamps, glass lanterns, and decorative objects adorned with Islamic motifs, which add a touch of elegance and spirituality to any home.

8. Tips for Shopping for Unique Souvenirs:

Explore Granada's local markets, artisan workshops, and boutique shops to discover unique and authentic souvenirs that reflect the city's culture and heritage.

Don't be afraid to haggle with vendors, especially at markets and craft fairs, where bargaining is a common practice and can lead to better deals and discounts.

Consider the size, weight, and fragility of souvenirs when purchasing them, especially if you plan to transport them back home in your luggage or carry-on.

In summary, Granada offers a diverse array of unique souvenirs that capture the essence of this captivating city, from Moorish-inspired crafts and handwoven textiles to Andalusian ceramics and local delicacies. Whether you're seeking a decorative keepsake, a culinary treat, or a musical memento, Granada's souvenirs provide travelers with lasting memories of their journey to this enchanting corner of Andalusia.

6.0 Cuisine and Dining

6.1 Local Granada Dishes

Granada, nestled in the heart of Andalusia, boasts a rich culinary heritage shaped by its diverse history, fertile lands, and vibrant culture. From traditional Moorish recipes to modern Spanish fusion cuisine, Granada's local dishes reflect the region's agricultural abundance, culinary creativity, and cultural influences. Here's an extensive guide to some of the most iconic and delicious dishes you can savor in Granada:

1. Tapas:

Granada is renowned for its tapas culture, where small plates of food are served with drinks in bars and taverns, creating a social and convivial atmosphere.

Traditional tapas in Granada include classics such as patatas bravas (fried potatoes with spicy tomato sauce), croquetas (croquettes filled with ham or cheese), albóndigas (meatballs in tomato sauce), and tortilla española (Spanish omelet with potatoes and onions).

Many bars and restaurants in Granada offer complimentary tapas with each drink order, allowing diners to sample a variety of flavors and specialties without breaking the bank.

2. Gazpacho Andaluz:

Gazpacho Andaluz is a refreshing cold soup made with ripe tomatoes, cucumbers, bell peppers, onions, garlic, olive oil, vinegar, and bread, blended to a smooth consistency and served chilled.

This classic Andalusian dish is perfect for hot summer days, offering a burst of flavor and a healthy dose of vitamins and antioxidants.

In Granada, gazpacho Andaluz is often garnished with diced vegetables, croutons, and a drizzle of olive oil, adding texture and richness to this iconic dish.

3. Piononos:

Piononos are sweet pastries native to Granada, consisting of a thin layer of sponge cake rolled around a creamy filling, typically made with custard, cream, or dulce de leche.

These bite-sized delights are then dusted with powdered sugar and cinnamon, creating a deliciously sweet and indulgent treat.

Piononos are a popular dessert in Granada and can be found in bakeries, pastry shops, and cafes throughout the city, making them the perfect souvenir to bring home to share with friends and family.

4. Plato Alpujarreño:

The Plato Alpujarreño is a hearty and flavorful dish originating from the Alpujarra region of Granada, characterized by its mountainous terrain and fertile valleys.

This rustic dish typically includes a combination of local ingredients such as morcilla (blood sausage), chorizo, fried eggs, potatoes, peppers, and ham, all cooked together in a sizzling skillet.
The Plato Alpujarreño showcases the region's abundance of fresh produce,

traditional charcuterie, and hearty mountain fare, making it a must-try for visitors looking to experience the flavors of Granada's countryside.

5. Habas con Jamón:

Habas con jamón is a simple yet delicious dish made with fresh broad beans (habas) sautéed with cured ham (jamón), onions, garlic, olive oil, and a splash of white wine.

This traditional Andalusian dish highlights the region's seasonal ingredients and culinary traditions, with the sweetness of the beans complementing the savory richness of the ham.

Habas con jamón is often served as a tapa or side dish, accompanied by crusty bread and a glass of local wine, providing a satisfying and flavorful culinary experience.

6. Migas:

Migas is a rustic dish made with leftover bread crumbs, typically seasoned with garlic, paprika, olive oil, and salt, then fried until crispy and golden brown.

In Granada, migas are often served with a variety of accompaniments such as fried eggs, chorizo, peppers, and grapes, adding texture and flavor to this simple yet satisfying dish.

Migas is a popular comfort food in Granada, especially during the colder months, offering warmth, nourishment, and a taste of traditional Andalusian cuisine.

7. Tips for Sampling Local Dishes:

Explore Granada's tapas bars and restaurants to sample a variety of traditional dishes and regional specialties, from classic tapas to innovative fusion cuisine.

Don't be afraid to ask locals for recommendations or try unfamiliar dishes, as Granada's culinary scene offers a wealth of flavors and experiences waiting to be discovered.

Consider joining a food tour or cooking class to learn more about Granada's culinary traditions, ingredients, and techniques, while enjoying hands-on experiences and tastings led by local experts.

In summary, Granada's local dishes offer a delicious journey through the region's culinary heritage, from tapas and soups to pastries and hearty mountain fare. Whether you're savoring classic tapas in a bustling bar or indulging in sweet treats from a local bakery, Granada's food scene promises a feast for the senses and memories to last a lifetime.

6.2 Popular Restaurants and Cafes

Granada, with its rich culinary heritage and vibrant food scene, offers visitors a diverse array of dining options, from traditional tapas bars and family-run restaurants to trendy cafes and innovative eateries. Whether you're craving authentic Andalusian cuisine, international flavors, or creative fusion dishes, Granada has something to satisfy every palate. Here's an extensive guide to some of the most popular restaurants and cafes in Granada:

1. Los Diamantes:

Known for its fresh seafood and classic tapas, Los Diamantes is a beloved institution in Granada, with several locations throughout the city.

The restaurant's signature dish is the fried fish tapa, featuring a variety of fresh catch served crispy and hot alongside a glass of cold beer or wine.

Other popular tapas at Los Diamantes include grilled octopus, shrimp skewers, marinated sardines, and seafood paella, all prepared with quality ingredients and expert culinary skill.

2. Bar La Tana:

Tucked away in the Albaicín neighborhood, Bar La Tana is a cozy and charming wine bar known for its excellent selection of Spanish wines and gourmet tapas.

The bar offers a rotating menu of seasonal tapas made with locally sourced ingredients, including artisanal cheeses, cured meats, olives, and preserves.

Visitors can relax on the outdoor terrace or cozy up inside the rustic interior, sipping on fine wines and savoring the flavors of Andalusia in a relaxed and convivial atmosphere.

3. Restaurante Arrayanes:

Situated in the historic Albaicín district, Restaurante Arrayanes offers a romantic setting and stunning views of the Alhambra, making it a popular choice for special occasions and romantic dinners.

The restaurant specializes in traditional Andalusian cuisine with a modern twist, featuring dishes such as grilled meats, seafood paella, and vegetable tagines, all prepared with seasonal ingredients and innovative flair.

Guests can dine in the elegant dining room or on the outdoor terrace, enjoying impeccable service, exquisite cuisine, and panoramic views of Granada's iconic landmarks.

4. Café Baraka:

Nestled in the Albaicín neighborhood, Café Baraka is a cozy and eclectic café known for its relaxed atmosphere, friendly service, and delicious vegetarian and vegan dishes.
The café offers a variety of healthy and flavorful options, including salads, sandwiches, wraps, and smoothies, made with organic ingredients and locally sourced produce.
Visitors can unwind on the outdoor patio, surrounded by lush greenery and colorful décor, while enjoying live music performances, art exhibitions, and cultural events hosted by the café.

5. Restaurante Ruta del Azafrán:

Located in the heart of Granada's historic center, Restaurante Ruta del Azafrán is a hidden gem known for its creative Andalusian cuisine and elegant ambiance.

The restaurant offers a seasonal menu inspired by traditional recipes and local ingredients, with dishes such as Iberian pork cheeks, Andalusian gazpacho, and almond-crusted fish, all artfully presented and bursting with flavor.

Guests can dine in the stylish dining room or on the outdoor terrace, enjoying attentive service, fine wines, and a culinary journey through the flavors of Granada and Andalusia.

6. Café Futbol:

A popular spot for coffee, breakfast, and brunch, Café Futbol is a cozy café located near Plaza Nueva, offering a laid-back atmosphere and friendly service.
The café serves a variety of coffee drinks, freshly baked pastries, sandwiches, and breakfast items, making it a favorite destination for locals and travelers looking

for a casual and affordable dining experience.

Visitors can relax on the outdoor terrace, people-watch, and soak in the bustling energy of Granada's city center while enjoying a leisurely meal or coffee break at Café Futbol.

7. Tips for Dining Out in Granada:

Make reservations in advance, especially for popular restaurants and during peak dining hours, to ensure a table and avoid long waits.

Be adventurous and try local specialties and seasonal dishes, as Granada's culinary scene offers a wealth of flavors and experiences waiting to be discovered.

Explore different neighborhoods and dining districts in Granada, from the historic Albaicín and Sacromonte to the bustling city center and trendy Realejo, to discover hidden gems and local favorites off the beaten path.

In summary, Granada's popular restaurants and cafes offer a diverse and delicious culinary landscape, showcasing the region's rich gastronomic traditions and creative innovations. Whether you're indulging in traditional tapas, savoring gourmet cuisine, or enjoying a leisurely coffee break, dining out in Granada promises a memorable and flavorful experience for every palate.

6.3 Street Food Experiences

Granada's vibrant streets are not only adorned with historic architecture and cultural landmarks but also bustling with the aromas and flavors of its delicious street food offerings. From traditional tapas to international delights, Granada's street food scene offers a diverse array of culinary experiences that are sure to tantalize your taste buds. Here's an extensive guide to savoring street food in Granada:

1. Bocadillos de Calamares:

A popular street food staple in Granada, bocadillos de calamares are crispy fried calamari sandwiches served in crusty bread rolls.

These savory sandwiches are typically served with a squeeze of lemon and a dollop of aioli or spicy salsa, adding a burst of flavor to each bite.

Visitors can find bocadillos de calamares at street stalls, food trucks, and traditional tapas bars throughout the city, especially in popular areas such as Plaza Nueva and Calle Navas.

2. Churros con Chocolate:

No visit to Granada is complete without indulging in churros con chocolate, a beloved Spanish treat enjoyed for breakfast, dessert, or as a late-night snack.

Churros are crispy fried dough pastries dusted with sugar and cinnamon, served with a cup of thick, rich chocolate dipping sauce for dunking.

Visitors can find churros con chocolate at street vendors, churrerías, and cafés across Granada, especially in the morning hours when locals gather to enjoy this delicious tradition.

3. Pinchos Morunos:

Pinchos morunos are flavorful skewers of marinated meat, typically pork or chicken, grilled to perfection and served with a side of bread or potatoes.

These savory snacks are seasoned with a blend of spices such as cumin, paprika, garlic, and herbs, imparting a rich and aromatic flavor to the tender meat.

Pinchos morunos are a popular street food option in Granada, often served at outdoor markets, festivals, and tapas bars, where visitors can enjoy them hot off the grill with a cold beer or glass of wine.

4. Tostas de Jamón y Queso:

Tostas de jamón y queso are open-faced sandwiches topped with thinly sliced cured ham (jamón) and melted cheese, served on toasted bread.

These simple yet satisfying snacks highlight the quality of Granada's local ingredients, with the rich flavor of the ham complemented by the creamy texture of the cheese and the crunch of the toast.

Visitors can find tostas de jamón y queso at street food stalls, market vendors, and tapas bars throughout Granada, making them a convenient and delicious option for a quick bite on the go.

5. Empanadas:

Empanadas are savory turnovers filled with a variety of delicious fillings, such as meat, vegetables, cheese, or seafood, encased in a flaky pastry crust.

These portable and satisfying snacks are perfect for enjoying on the go, whether you're exploring Granada's historic streets, strolling through the Albaicín neighborhood, or picnicking in one of the city's scenic parks.

Visitors can find empanadas at bakeries, street food markets, and specialty shops across Granada, with a wide range of flavors and fillings to suit every taste.

6. Tips for Enjoying Street Food Experiences:

Embrace the local culture and customs by sampling a variety of street food specialties, from traditional tapas to international flavors, to discover new tastes and culinary delights.

Be adventurous and try dishes that may be unfamiliar to you, as Granada's street food scene offers a wealth of unique and delicious options waiting to be discovered.

Explore different neighborhoods and districts in Granada to find hidden gems and local favorites off the beaten path, from bustling markets and food stalls to quaint cafes and bakeries.

In summary, Granada's street food scene offers a delicious array of flavors and experiences, from classic Spanish treats to international delights, providing visitors with a convenient and enjoyable way to sample the city's culinary heritage on the go. Whether you're indulging in crispy calamari sandwiches, dunking churros in thick chocolate sauce, or savoring savory skewers of marinated meat, street food in

Granada promises a flavorful adventure for every palate.

7.0 Exploring Granada

7.1 Alhambra Palace

The Alhambra Palace, perched atop a hill overlooking the city of Granada, stands as a testament to the rich history, exquisite craftsmanship, and cultural legacy of Moorish Spain. This architectural masterpiece, with its intricate carvings, stunning gardens, and breathtaking views, offers visitors a glimpse into the opulence and splendor of the Nasrid dynasty and the Islamic Golden Age. Here's an extensive guide to exploring the Alhambra Palace:

1. History and Origins:

The Alhambra Palace, originally built as a fortress in the 9th century during the Moorish occupation of Spain, was later converted into a royal palace and citadel by the Nasrid emirs in the 13th and 14th centuries.

Over the centuries, the Alhambra underwent several expansions and renovations, with successive rulers adding new palaces, fortifications, and gardens, resulting in the complex architectural ensemble that exists today.

After the Reconquista of Spain in 1492, the Catholic Monarchs, Ferdinand and Isabella, took control of the Alhambra and made it their royal residence, preserving and enhancing its beauty while incorporating Christian elements into its design.

2. Architectural Wonders:

The Alhambra Palace is renowned for its stunning architectural features, including intricate stucco work, carved wooden ceilings, and geometric tile patterns, which adorn its palaces, halls, and courtyards.
Highlights of the palace complex include the Nasrid Palaces, with their elaborate chambers, courtyards, and reflecting pools, such as the iconic Court of the Lions and the majestic Hall of the Ambassadors.
The Alhambra also boasts the Alcazaba, the oldest part of the complex, which served as a military fortress with defensive walls, towers, and commanding views of the surrounding countryside.

Visitors can explore the Generalife Gardens, a series of lush green spaces, fountains, and terraces, which served as a retreat for the Nasrid rulers and offer stunning panoramic views of Granada and the Sierra Nevada mountains.

3. Cultural Significance:

The Alhambra Palace is recognized as a UNESCO World Heritage Site and is considered one of the greatest architectural treasures of the Islamic world, attracting millions of visitors from around the globe each year.
Its exquisite blend of Islamic, Christian, and Moorish influences reflects the diverse cultural heritage of Spain and serves as a symbol of tolerance, coexistence, and artistic expression.

The Alhambra has inspired countless poets, artists, and writers over the centuries, including Washington Irving, whose book "Tales of the Alhambra" helped popularize the palace's mystique and allure in the Western world.

Today, the Alhambra continues to captivate visitors with its beauty, history, and spirituality, offering a unique and unforgettable experience that transcends time and culture.

4. Visitor Experience:

Due to its popularity and limited capacity, it's essential for visitors to book tickets to the Alhambra Palace well in advance, especially during peak tourist seasons.

Guided tours are available for those who wish to learn more about the history, architecture, and significance of the palace complex, offering insights and perspectives from knowledgeable local guides.

Visitors should plan to spend several hours exploring the Alhambra at a leisurely pace, allowing ample time to admire its architectural details, stroll through its gardens, and soak in its serene atmosphere.
Audio guides and informational materials are available in multiple languages to enhance the visitor experience and provide context and interpretation of the palace's many features and attractions.

5. Preservation and Conservation:

The preservation and conservation of the Alhambra Palace are of utmost importance to ensure its continued beauty and cultural significance for future generations.

Ongoing restoration efforts, research projects, and maintenance work are carried out by dedicated teams of architects, historians, and conservationists to safeguard the palace's structural integrity and artistic heritage.

Sustainable tourism practices, such as visitor management strategies, environmental protection measures, and community engagement initiatives, are implemented to minimize the impact of tourism on the fragile ecosystem and cultural landscape of the Alhambra.

In summary, the Alhambra Palace stands as a timeless symbol of Granada's rich history, architectural splendor, and cultural legacy, inviting visitors to embark on a journey through the past and experience the beauty and wonder of Moorish Spain. Whether marveling at its intricate carvings, wandering through its lush gardens, or contemplating its panoramic views, a visit to the Alhambra is sure to leave a lasting impression and create cherished memories for a lifetime.

7.2 Generalife Gardens

Nestled within the magnificent Alhambra complex in Granada, the Generalife Gardens stand as a verdant testament to the Islamic influence on Andalusian landscape design. These lush gardens, with their intricately designed terraces, fragrant blooms, and serene water features, offer visitors a tranquil retreat from the bustling city below. Here's an extensive exploration of the Generalife Gardens:

1. Origins and History:

The Generalife Gardens, originally known as the "Jannat al-'Arif" or "Architect's Garden," were created in the 13th century as a private retreat for the Nasrid rulers of Granada.
Designed to provide respite and relaxation for the royal family, the gardens were meticulously planned to evoke the idea of

paradise on earth, with their harmonious blend of architecture, water, and vegetation.

Over the centuries, the Generalife Gardens underwent several renovations and expansions, with successive rulers adding new elements and features to enhance their beauty and functionality.

2. Architectural Features:

The Generalife Gardens are characterized by their terraced layout, with a series of interconnected courtyards, pathways, and pavilions that lead visitors on a journey through nature and tranquility.

The gardens are adorned with fountains, pools, and water channels, which create a soothing ambiance and reflect the Islamic belief in the importance of water as a symbol of life and purity.

The iconic Water Staircase, with its cascading fountains and lush greenery, is one of the most picturesque spots in the Generalife Gardens, offering stunning views of the Alhambra Palace and the city of Granada beyond.

3. Flora and Fauna:

The Generalife Gardens boast a diverse array of plant species, including fragrant roses, colorful bougainvillea, aromatic jasmine, and lush citrus trees, which fill the air with their sweet scents and vibrant hues.

The gardens are carefully landscaped to showcase a variety of textures, colors, and seasonal blooms, providing a feast for the senses and a peaceful sanctuary for visitors to explore and enjoy.

Wildlife such as birds, butterflies, and bees can be spotted flitting among the flowers and foliage, adding to the natural beauty and biodiversity of the Generalife Gardens.

4. Architectural Elements:

In addition to its lush vegetation, the Generalife Gardens feature several architectural elements, including pavilions, pergolas, and arched walkways, which provide shade, shelter, and visual interest throughout the gardens.

The Patio de la Acequia (Court of the Water Channel) is a central feature of the Generalife Gardens, with its long, narrow pool flanked by cypress trees and surrounded by symmetrical flower beds, creating a serene and harmonious space for contemplation.

Visitors can also explore the Sultana's Court, a secluded courtyard with a central fountain and shady alcoves, which served as a private retreat for the Nasrid queens and their attendants.

5. Visitor Experience:

The Generalife Gardens are open to visitors year-round, offering a peaceful escape from the crowds and heat of the Alhambra Palace, especially during the hot summer months.
Guided tours are available for those who wish to learn more about the history, design, and significance of the gardens, providing insights and perspectives from knowledgeable local guides.

Visitors are encouraged to take their time exploring the Generalife Gardens, strolling along its shaded pathways, admiring its architectural features, and pausing to enjoy the beauty and tranquility of this enchanting oasis.

6. Preservation and Conservation:

The preservation and conservation of the Generalife Gardens are of utmost importance to ensure their continued beauty and cultural significance for future generations.
Ongoing restoration efforts, landscaping projects, and maintenance work are carried out by dedicated teams of gardeners, architects, and conservationists to safeguard the gardens' historical integrity and natural beauty.

Sustainable gardening practices, such as water conservation measures, organic pest control methods, and native plant restoration initiatives, are implemented to minimize the environmental impact of maintaining the Generalife Gardens.

In summary, the Generalife Gardens stand as a timeless masterpiece of Islamic landscape design, offering visitors a serene and enchanting retreat from the hustle and bustle of modern life. Whether wandering among its fragrant blooms, lounging by its tranquil pools, or marveling at its architectural wonders, a visit to the Generalife Gardens is sure to leave a lasting impression and create cherished memories of Granada's natural beauty and cultural heritage.

7.3 Nasrid Palaces

The Nasrid Palaces, nestled within the majestic Alhambra complex in Granada, Spain, stand as a pinnacle of Moorish architecture and artistic achievement. These exquisite palaces, with their intricate carvings, ornate tilework, and serene courtyards, offer visitors a rare glimpse into the opulent lifestyle and refined taste of the Nasrid dynasty, who ruled over Granada during the Islamic Golden Age. Here's an extensive exploration of the Nasrid Palaces:

1. Historical Significance:

The Nasrid Palaces were constructed during the 13th and 14th centuries as the royal residences of the Nasrid emirs, who governed the Emirate of Granada from the Alhambra complex.

The palaces served as the seat of power and prestige for the Nasrid dynasty, providing a luxurious and secure haven for the ruling family, their courtiers, and their guests.

Despite the political upheavals and dynastic struggles that characterized the later years of Nasrid rule, the palaces remained a symbol of Moorish sovereignty and cultural identity until the Christian Reconquista of Spain in 1492.

2. Architectural Marvels:

The Nasrid Palaces are renowned for their exquisite architecture, characterized by their intricate stucco work, geometric tile patterns, and delicate filigree carvings, which adorn their walls, ceilings, and arches.

Each palace within the complex, including the Mexuar, the Comares Palace, and the Palace of the Lions, features its own unique architectural style and decorative motifs, reflecting the evolving tastes and influences of the Nasrid rulers.

Highlights of the Nasrid Palaces include the iconic Court of the Lions, with its magnificent marble fountain and intricately carved columns, and the Hall of the Ambassadors, with its stunning dome ceiling and panoramic views of Granada.

3. Symbolism and Spirituality:

The design and layout of the Nasrid Palaces were deeply influenced by Islamic principles of symmetry, harmony, and spiritual symbolism, which are evident in their geometric patterns, water features, and garden courtyards.

Water, in particular, played a central role in the design of the palaces, symbolizing purity, fertility, and the abundance of paradise, as described in Islamic texts and poetry.

Visitors to the Nasrid Palaces can experience a sense of tranquility and serenity as they wander through the labyrinthine corridors, lush gardens, and sunlit courtyards, marveling at the beauty and craftsmanship of their surroundings.

4. Artistic Legacy:

The Nasrid Palaces are a testament to the artistic genius and cultural sophistication of the Nasrid dynasty, who patronized some of the most talented craftsmen, artisans, and architects of their time.

The intricate carvings, colorful tilework, and elaborate plasterwork found throughout the palaces reflect the diverse influences of Islamic, Christian, and Jewish artistic traditions, creating a unique fusion of styles and techniques.

The Nasrid Palaces inspired generations of artists, architects, and scholars, including Washington Irving, whose writings helped popularize the Alhambra complex and its enchanting palaces in the Western world.

5. Visitor Experience:

Visiting the Nasrid Palaces is a highlight of any trip to Granada, offering visitors a rare opportunity to step back in time and immerse themselves in the grandeur and splendor of Moorish Spain.

Due to their popularity and limited capacity, it's essential for visitors to book tickets to the Nasrid Palaces well in advance, especially during peak tourist seasons.

Guided tours are available for those who wish to learn more about the history, architecture, and significance of the palaces, providing insights and perspectives from knowledgeable local guides.

6. Preservation and Conservation:

The preservation and conservation of the Nasrid Palaces are of utmost importance to ensure their continued beauty and cultural significance for future generations.
Ongoing restoration efforts, research projects, and maintenance work are carried out by dedicated teams of architects, historians, and conservationists to safeguard the palaces' structural integrity and artistic heritage.

Sustainable tourism practices, such as visitor management strategies, environmental protection measures, and community engagement initiatives, are implemented to minimize the impact of tourism on the fragile ecosystem and cultural landscape of the Nasrid Palaces.

In summary, the Nasrid Palaces stand as a timeless testament to the splendor and sophistication of Moorish civilization, offering visitors a glimpse into the rich history, artistic legacy, and cultural heritage of Granada and Andalusia. Whether marveling at their intricate carvings, strolling through their lush gardens, or contemplating their spiritual symbolism, a visit to the Nasrid Palaces is sure to leave a lasting impression and create cherished memories of Moorish Spain's golden age.

7.4 Alcazaba Fortress

The Alcazaba Fortress, situated within the grand Alhambra complex in Granada, Spain, stands as a formidable symbol of Moorish military prowess and strategic ingenuity. As the oldest section of the Alhambra, this ancient fortress offers visitors a glimpse into the defensive architecture and military history of Islamic Spain. Here's an extensive exploration of the Alcazaba Fortress:

1. Historical Significance:

The Alcazaba Fortress was originally constructed in the 9th century during the early Muslim rule of Spain, serving as a military stronghold and defensive bastion against invading forces.
Strategically positioned atop a hill overlooking the city of Granada and the surrounding countryside, the fortress provided a commanding vantage point from which to monitor and protect the region.
Over the centuries, the Alcazaba underwent several renovations and expansions under successive rulers, including the Nasrid emirs, who transformed it into a royal residence and administrative center.

2. Architectural Marvels:

The Alcazaba Fortress is characterized by its robust defensive walls, towering watchtowers, and imposing gateways, which were designed to withstand siege warfare and protect the inhabitants within.

The fortress features a series of interconnected courtyards, barracks, and storage facilities, arranged in a strategic layout to optimize defensive capabilities and troop movements.

Highlights of the Alcazaba include the Torre de la Vela (Watchtower), which offers panoramic views of Granada and the surrounding countryside, and the Torre Quebrada (Broken Tower), which served as a defensive bastion during medieval battles.

3. Strategic Importance:

The Alcazaba Fortress played a crucial role in the defense of Granada and the surrounding region during the medieval period, serving as a stronghold against Christian incursions from the north.

Its elevated position and fortified walls provided a secure refuge for the ruling elite, military garrison, and civilian population in times of conflict, allowing them to withstand prolonged sieges and maintain control over the territory.
The fortress also served as a symbol of Moorish sovereignty and cultural identity, reflecting the power and prestige of the Nasrid dynasty and its predecessors.

4. Visitor Experience:

Visiting the Alcazaba Fortress offers visitors a unique opportunity to step back in time

and explore the military history and architectural heritage of Islamic Spain.
Guided tours are available for those who wish to learn more about the history, architecture, and significance of the fortress, providing insights and perspectives from knowledgeable local guides.

Visitors can climb the steep staircases, wander through the ancient courtyards, and ascend the watchtowers of the Alcazaba, imagining themselves as defenders of the realm amidst the echoes of centuries past.

5. Preservation and Conservation:

The preservation and conservation of the Alcazaba Fortress are of utmost importance to ensure its continued beauty and historical significance for future generations.
Ongoing restoration efforts, archaeological excavations, and maintenance work are

carried out by dedicated teams of historians, architects, and conservationists to safeguard the fortress's structural integrity and cultural heritage.

Sustainable tourism practices, such as visitor management strategies, environmental protection measures, and community engagement initiatives, are implemented to minimize the impact of tourism on the fragile ecosystem and cultural landscape of the Alcazaba Fortress.

In summary, the Alcazaba Fortress stands as a testament to the strength, resilience, and ingenuity of Moorish civilization, offering visitors a glimpse into the military history and architectural legacy of Islamic Spain. Whether marveling at its imposing walls, exploring its ancient courtyards, or admiring its panoramic views, a visit to the Alcazaba Fortress is sure to leave a lasting impression and create cherished memories of Granada's rich heritage.

7.5 Granada Cathedral

The Granada Cathedral, also known as the Cathedral of the Incarnation (Catedral de la Encarnación), stands as a grand symbol of Christian triumph and architectural splendor in the heart of Granada, Spain. This majestic cathedral, with its imposing façade, soaring vaulted ceilings, and ornate chapels, is a masterpiece of Renaissance architecture and a testament to the city's rich religious and cultural heritage. Here's an extensive exploration of the Granada Cathedral:

1. Historical Background:

Construction of the Granada Cathedral began in the early 16th century, following the Reconquista of Spain by Catholic Monarchs Ferdinand and Isabella in 1492.

Built atop the site of the former Great Mosque of Granada, the cathedral was intended to showcase the power and prestige of the newly established Christian kingdom and serve as a center of worship for the faithful.

The cathedral's construction spanned several centuries, with different architects and craftsmen contributing to its design and embellishment, resulting in a unique blend of Gothic, Renaissance, and Baroque styles.

2. Architectural Features:

The Granada Cathedral is renowned for its impressive façade, adorned with intricate stone carvings, sculptural reliefs, and towering spires that reach towards the heavens.
The interior of the cathedral is equally awe-inspiring, with its soaring vaulted ceilings, majestic columns, and magnificent altarpieces, including the main altarpiece, crafted by renowned sculptor Alonso Cano.

The cathedral's chapels are adorned with exquisite works of art, including paintings, sculptures, and religious relics, by renowned artists such as El Greco, Alonso Cano, and Juan de Medina.

3. Iconic Elements:

One of the most iconic features of the Granada Cathedral is its Royal Chapel (Capilla Real), which houses the tombs of Queen Isabella I of Castile, King Ferdinand II of Aragon, and their descendants.

The Royal Chapel is a masterpiece of Renaissance architecture, with its elaborate marble tombs, intricately carved choir stalls, and magnificent altarpieces, creating a solemn and majestic space for prayer and reflection.

Another notable element of the cathedral is its Sacristy (Sagrario), a lavishly decorated space filled with ornate woodwork, gilded altars, and exquisite religious artifacts, including a collection of precious silverware and liturgical vestments.

4. Cultural Significance:

The Granada Cathedral is a UNESCO World Heritage Site and is considered one of the most important religious and architectural landmarks in Spain, attracting millions of visitors from around the world each year.

Beyond its religious significance, the cathedral has played a central role in the cultural and social life of Granada, hosting religious ceremonies, artistic performances, and community events throughout its long history.

The cathedral's rich artistic heritage and cultural legacy have inspired generations of artists, architects, and scholars, contributing to the preservation and appreciation of Spain's artistic and architectural heritage.

5. Visitor Experience:

Visiting the Granada Cathedral offers visitors a unique opportunity to immerse themselves in the history, art, and spirituality of this magnificent monument.

Guided tours are available for those who wish to learn more about the cathedral's history, architecture, and significance, providing insights and perspectives from knowledgeable local guides.

Visitors can explore the cathedral at their own pace, admiring its architectural details, studying its artistic treasures, and experiencing the sense of awe and reverence that pervades its sacred spaces.

6. Preservation and Conservation:

The preservation and conservation of the Granada Cathedral are of utmost importance to ensure its continued beauty and cultural significance for future generations.
Ongoing restoration efforts, maintenance work, and research projects are carried out by dedicated teams of architects, historians, and conservationists to safeguard the cathedral's structural integrity and artistic heritage.

Sustainable tourism practices, such as visitor management strategies, environmental protection measures, and community engagement initiatives, are implemented to minimize the impact of tourism on the fragile ecosystem and cultural landscape of the Granada Cathedral.

In summary, the Granada Cathedral stands as a timeless testament to the power of faith, the beauty of art, and the enduring legacy of Spain's rich religious and cultural heritage. Whether marveling at its majestic façade, exploring its sacred spaces, or admiring its artistic treasures, a visit to the Granada Cathedral is sure to inspire awe and reverence for centuries to come.

7.6 Albayzín District

The Albayzín district, nestled on the hillside opposite the Alhambra in Granada, Spain, is a captivating labyrinth of narrow streets, whitewashed houses, and ancient landmarks that bear witness to the city's rich and diverse history. This UNESCO World Heritage Site is renowned for its Moorish architecture, Islamic heritage, and vibrant cultural scene, making it a must-visit destination for travelers seeking an authentic and immersive experience in Granada. Here's an extensive exploration of the Albayzín district:

1. Historical Background:

The Albayzín district traces its origins back to the Nasrid period of Moorish rule in Spain, when it served as the residential quarter for Granada's Muslim population.
Originally known as "Medina al-Bayyazin" or "the White City," the Albayzín was characterized by its whitewashed houses, narrow alleyways, and traditional Moorish architecture, which reflected the cultural and architectural influences of Al-Andalus.
Following the Christian Reconquista of Granada in 1492, the Albayzín underwent significant changes, as Christian settlers moved into the area and repurposed many of its Islamic buildings for their own use.

2. Architectural Marvels:

The Albayzín district is renowned for its stunning Moorish architecture, with highlights including the historic mosques, minarets, and carmenes (traditional Moorish houses) that dot its winding streets and alleyways.

One of the most iconic landmarks in the Albayzín is the Church of San Nicolás, which offers panoramic views of the Alhambra and the Sierra Nevada mountains from its elevated terrace.

Other notable architectural features of the Albayzín include the Puerta de Elvira, an ancient gate that once served as the main entrance to the city, and the Dar al-Horra Palace, the former residence of the mother of Boabdil, the last Nasrid ruler of Granada.

3. Cultural Heritage:

The Albayzín district is a melting pot of cultures and traditions, where Islamic, Christian, and Jewish influences coexist harmoniously, reflecting the diverse history and heritage of Granada.

Visitors to the Albayzín can explore its narrow streets and hidden squares, where artisans, musicians, and street performers showcase the vibrant cultural scene of the district.

The Albayzín is also home to a thriving community of artists, writers, and intellectuals, who draw inspiration from its historic surroundings and picturesque landscapes.

4. Culinary Delights:

The Albayzín district boasts a wealth of traditional tapas bars, teahouses, and restaurants where visitors can savor the flavors of Andalusian cuisine.

Popular dishes in the Albayzín include traditional Spanish tapas such as patatas bravas, jamón ibérico, and tortilla española, as well as Moorish-inspired specialties like tagines, couscous, and pastelas.

Visitors can also sample traditional Moroccan tea and pastries at the district's many teahouses and cafés, which offer a relaxing atmosphere and stunning views of the Alhambra.

5. Vibrant Community Life:

The Albayzín district is known for its vibrant community life, with residents gathering in its squares and plazas for cultural events, festivals, and celebrations throughout the year.

One of the most famous events in the Albayzín is the Festival of San Cecilio, held in February, which celebrates the patron saint of Granada with music, dance, and religious processions.

Other cultural highlights of the Albayzín include the Flamenco Festival, which showcases the traditional music and dance of Andalusia, and the International Festival of Music and Dance, which attracts world-renowned performers to the district's historic venues.

6. Preservation and Conservation:

The preservation and conservation of the Albayzín district are of utmost importance to ensure its continued beauty and cultural significance for future generations.

Ongoing restoration efforts, maintenance work, and community engagement initiatives are carried out by local authorities, heritage organizations, and residents to safeguard the district's architectural heritage and historic character.

Sustainable tourism practices, such as visitor management strategies, environmental protection measures, and heritage education programs, are implemented to minimize the impact of tourism on the Albayzín's fragile ecosystem and cultural landscape.

In summary, the Albayzín district is a treasure trove of history, culture, and charm, where visitors can immerse themselves in the rich tapestry of Granada's past and present. Whether wandering through its ancient streets, marveling at its architectural wonders, or savoring its culinary delights, a visit to the Albayzín promises an unforgettable journey through the heart and soul of Andalusia.

8.0 Outdoor Adventures

8.1 Sierra Nevada National Park

Sierra Nevada National Park, located in the southern Spanish region of Andalusia, is a breathtaking wilderness of rugged mountains, pristine forests, and crystal-clear rivers. This UNESCO Biosphere Reserve is renowned for its stunning natural beauty, rich biodiversity, and unique cultural heritage, making it a popular destination for outdoor enthusiasts, nature lovers, and adventure seekers. Here's an extensive exploration of the Sierra Nevada National Park:

1. Geological and Geographic Features:

Sierra Nevada National Park is home to the highest mountain range in mainland Spain, with peaks reaching over 3,400 meters above sea level, including the iconic Mulhacén, the highest peak in the Iberian Peninsula.

The park encompasses a diverse range of landscapes, from snow-capped summits and alpine meadows to deep valleys, rocky gorges, and lush forests of oak, pine, and fir. The park's geology is characterized by granite and limestone formations, glacial valleys, and karst landscapes, which have been shaped by millions of years of geological activity and erosion.

2. Flora and Fauna:

Sierra Nevada National Park is a biodiversity hotspot, with over 2,100 plant species and a rich array of wildlife, including rare and endangered species such as the Iberian ibex, Spanish ibex, and Spanish imperial eagle.

The park's diverse habitats support a wide range of flora and fauna, from alpine flowers and mountain herbs to birds of prey, mammals, and reptiles adapted to life in the high mountains.

Endemic species, such as the Sierra Nevada violet and the Sierra Nevada blue butterfly, are found nowhere else in the world, making the park a globally significant center of biodiversity and conservation.

3. Outdoor Activities:

Sierra Nevada National Park offers a wealth of outdoor activities for visitors to enjoy, including hiking, mountain biking, rock climbing, horseback riding, and wildlife watching.

The park is crisscrossed by a network of well-marked trails and footpaths that cater to hikers of all skill levels, from leisurely strolls through scenic valleys to challenging ascents of high mountain peaks.

During the winter months, Sierra Nevada becomes a popular destination for skiing, snowboarding, and other winter sports, with several ski resorts offering world-class facilities and stunning views of the surrounding mountains.

4. Cultural Heritage:

The Sierra Nevada region has a rich cultural heritage, with a history dating back thousands of years to the time of the Iberians, Romans, and Moors, who left their mark on the landscape through ancient settlements, fortifications, and irrigation systems.

The traditional villages and hamlets scattered throughout the park are home to a vibrant rural culture, where traditional customs, crafts, and festivals are still celebrated today.

The park's cultural heritage is also reflected in its cuisine, which features local specialties such as wild game, mountain cheeses, and hearty stews made with seasonal ingredients from the surrounding countryside.

5. Conservation and Management:

Sierra Nevada National Park is managed by the Andalusian Regional Government, in collaboration with local communities, conservation organizations, and other stakeholders.

Conservation efforts in the park focus on protecting its unique biodiversity, preserving its natural landscapes, and promoting sustainable tourism practices that minimize the impact on the environment.

Research and monitoring programs are conducted to study the park's flora and fauna, assess the effectiveness of conservation measures, and address emerging threats such as climate change, habitat loss, and invasive species.

6. Visitor Facilities and Services:

Sierra Nevada National Park offers a range of visitor facilities and services, including visitor centers, interpretation exhibits, camping areas, and mountain refuges.
Guided tours, educational programs, and outdoor activities are available for visitors of all ages, providing opportunities to learn about the park's natural and cultural heritage while enjoying its scenic beauty.

Information on trails, safety guidelines, and park regulations is provided to help visitors make the most of their experience while respecting the park's fragile ecosystems and wildlife.

In summary, Sierra Nevada National Park is a sanctuary of natural beauty and biodiversity, where visitors can immerse themselves in the majesty of the mountains, explore pristine wildernesses, and discover the rich cultural heritage of the Andalusian countryside. Whether hiking to high mountain peaks, skiing down snowy slopes, or simply admiring the panoramic views, a visit to Sierra Nevada promises an unforgettable journey through Spain's alpine paradise.

8.2 Skiing and Snowboarding

Sierra Nevada, located in the southern Spanish region of Andalusia, is not only renowned for its stunning natural beauty and rich biodiversity but also for offering some of the best skiing and snowboarding experiences in Europe. With its high-altitude peaks, abundant snowfall, and modern ski resorts, Sierra Nevada attracts winter sports enthusiasts from around the world who come to enjoy its pristine slopes, breathtaking scenery, and vibrant après-ski scene. Here's an extensive exploration of skiing and snowboarding in Sierra Nevada:

1. Ski Resorts and Facilities:

Sierra Nevada boasts one of Europe's most modern and well-equipped ski resorts, offering a wide range of facilities and amenities for skiers and snowboarders of all levels.

The main ski resort, also named Sierra Nevada, is located just a short drive from the city of Granada and offers easy access to the slopes via a network of lifts, gondolas, and chairlifts.

The resort features over 120 kilometers of ski runs, ranging from gentle beginner slopes to challenging black diamond runs, as well as terrain parks, halfpipes, and freestyle areas for snowboarders and freestyle skiers.

Ski and snowboard rental shops, ski schools, mountain restaurants, and après-ski bars are available throughout the resort, providing everything visitors need for a memorable winter sports experience.

2. Skiing and Snowboarding Terrain:

Sierra Nevada offers a diverse range of skiing and snowboarding terrain, with slopes and trails suitable for all skill levels, from absolute beginners to seasoned experts.

The resort's high-altitude location and favorable climate ensure excellent snow conditions throughout the winter season, with reliable snowfall from December to April and an average snow depth of over two meters.

Ski runs are groomed daily and maintained to the highest standards, providing smooth and well-marked trails for skiers and snowboarders to enjoy.
Off-piste skiing and snowboarding opportunities are also available for those seeking more challenging terrain, with guided tours and avalanche safety equipment recommended for exploring the backcountry.

3. Skiing and Snowboarding Lessons:

Sierra Nevada offers a variety of ski and snowboard lessons and programs for individuals and groups of all ages and abilities.

Professional instructors are available to teach beginners the basics of skiing and snowboarding, including proper technique, balance, and control, while experienced riders can take advanced lessons to improve their skills and tackle more challenging terrain.

Private lessons, group lessons, and multi-day courses are available, allowing visitors to tailor their learning experience to their specific needs and preferences.
Children's ski and snowboard programs are also offered, providing a fun and safe environment for kids to learn and develop their skills on the slopes.

4. Après-Ski and Nightlife:

After a day on the slopes, visitors can unwind and socialize at Sierra Nevada's vibrant après-ski scene, which offers a variety of bars, restaurants, and entertainment options.

The resort's mountain restaurants and chalets serve up delicious Andalusian cuisine, tapas, and drinks, allowing skiers and snowboarders to refuel and relax with stunning views of the surrounding mountains.

In the evenings, the resort comes alive with live music, DJs, and themed parties at its après-ski bars and clubs, where visitors can dance the night away and celebrate their day on the slopes.

5. Safety and Health Measures:

Sierra Nevada prioritizes the safety and well-being of its visitors and has implemented strict health and safety measures to prevent the spread of COVID-19 and ensure a safe skiing and snowboarding experience.

Enhanced cleaning and sanitation protocols are in place at all facilities, including ski lifts, rental shops, and mountain restaurants, with hand sanitizer stations available throughout the resort.

Social distancing measures, mask mandates, and capacity limits are enforced in indoor spaces and crowded areas, while advanced online booking and contactless payment options are encouraged to minimize contact and reduce the risk of transmission.

In summary, skiing and snowboarding in Sierra Nevada offer an unforgettable winter sports experience, with world-class facilities, stunning scenery, and a lively après-ski scene that cater to skiers and snowboarders of all levels and interests. Whether carving turns on the slopes, enjoying après-ski drinks with friends, or taking in the panoramic views of the mountains, a visit to

Sierra Nevada promises an exhilarating and memorable alpine adventure.

8.3 Hiking Trails

Sierra Nevada, located in the southern Spanish region of Andalusia, offers an extensive network of hiking trails that wind through its stunning landscapes, from rugged mountains and deep valleys to lush forests and alpine meadows. Whether you're a seasoned trekker seeking a challenging ascent to a high mountain peak or a leisurely hiker looking for a scenic stroll through nature, Sierra Nevada has a trail for you. Here's an extensive exploration of hiking trails in Sierra Nevada:

1. Mulhacén Summit Trail:

The Mulhacén Summit Trail is one of the most iconic and challenging hikes in Sierra Nevada, leading to the highest peak in mainland Spain, Mulhacén, which stands at 3,479 meters above sea level.

This demanding trek takes hikers through rugged terrain, rocky slopes, and high-altitude plateaus, offering breathtaking panoramic views of the surrounding mountains and valleys along the way.

The trail can be completed as a long day hike or as part of a multi-day trek, with options to camp overnight at designated campsites or mountain refuges along the route.

2. Vereda de la Estrella Trail:

The Vereda de la Estrella Trail, also known as the Path of the Star, is a popular hiking route that traverses the heart of Sierra

Nevada, offering stunning views of the surrounding peaks and valleys.

This moderate to challenging trail follows a well-marked path that winds through pine forests, alpine meadows, and rocky terrain, passing by mountain streams, waterfalls, and ancient ruins along the way.

The trail is best tackled as a full-day hike, with options to start and finish at various trailheads and access points throughout the park.

3. Río Genil Trail:

The Río Genil Trail follows the course of the Genil River as it meanders through the valleys and gorges of Sierra Nevada, offering hikers a scenic and tranquil journey through nature.

This easy to moderate trail passes through dense forests of oak, chestnut, and pine, with opportunities to spot wildlife such as deer, wild boar, and golden eagles along the way.

The trail is ideal for hikers of all skill levels and can be completed as a loop or out-and-back hike, with options to extend the route by exploring side trails and detours.

4. Los Cahorros Trail:

The Los Cahorros Trail is a thrilling and adventurous hike that takes hikers through a series of narrow gorges, suspension bridges, and natural rock formations in the foothills of Sierra Nevada.

This moderate to challenging trail offers a unique blend of natural beauty and adrenaline-pumping excitement, with opportunities to cross rushing rivers, scramble over boulders, and navigate tight passageways.

The trail is popular among thrill-seekers and outdoor enthusiasts, who come to test their skills and explore the rugged landscapes of Sierra Nevada's lesser-known valleys and canyons.

5. Sulayr Long-Distance Trail:

The Sulayr Long-Distance Trail, also known as the Circular Path of Sierra Nevada, is a 300-kilometer hiking route that circumnavigates the entire Sierra Nevada mountain range, offering hikers an epic adventure through some of the most remote and scenic landscapes in Andalusia.

This challenging trek takes approximately 15 to 20 days to complete and traverses a variety of terrain, including high mountain passes, alpine meadows, and rocky ridges, with opportunities to stay overnight at mountain refuges and campsites along the way.

The Sulayr Trail is divided into stages, each ranging from 10 to 20 kilometers in length, allowing hikers to customize their itinerary and choose the sections that best suit their skill level and interests.

6. Safety and Preparation:

Before embarking on any hike in Sierra Nevada, it's important to plan ahead, check the weather forecast, and familiarize yourself with the trail route, difficulty level, and elevation gain.
Proper hiking gear and equipment, including sturdy footwear, layers of clothing, a map, compass, and plenty of water and snacks, are essential for a safe and enjoyable hiking experience.
Hikers should also be aware of the potential hazards and risks associated with hiking in mountainous terrain, including sudden changes in weather, altitude sickness, and

wildlife encounters, and take appropriate precautions to mitigate these risks.

In summary, hiking in Sierra Nevada offers an unparalleled opportunity to explore the natural beauty, rich biodiversity, and rugged landscapes of one of Spain's most spectacular mountain ranges. Whether tackling a challenging ascent to a high mountain peak or enjoying a leisurely stroll through a scenic valley, hikers of all skill levels and interests are sure to find their perfect trail in Sierra Nevada.

8.4 Alpujarras Region

Nestled in the southern foothills of the Sierra Nevada mountain range, the Alpujarras region is a picturesque and enchanting area known for its stunning natural beauty, charming whitewashed villages, and rich cultural heritage. This rugged and mountainous landscape, dotted with terraced hillsides, ancient olive groves, and cascading rivers, has captivated travelers for centuries with its timeless allure and laid-back atmosphere. Here's an extensive exploration of the Alpujarras region:

1. Historical Background:

The Alpujarras region has a fascinating history that spans thousands of years, with evidence of human habitation dating back to prehistoric times.
During the medieval period, the Alpujarras was part of the Nasrid Kingdom of Granada, a last stronghold of Islamic rule in Spain before the Christian Reconquista.

After the fall of Granada in 1492, the Alpujarras became a refuge for the Moors who chose to remain in Spain and practice their religion and traditions in secret, giving rise to a unique cultural blend of Moorish and Christian influences that can still be seen today.

2. Scenic Landscapes:

The Alpujarras region is characterized by its rugged and mountainous terrain, with steep slopes, deep valleys, and terraced hillsides that are ideal for hiking, mountain biking, and outdoor exploration.

The region is also known for its diverse flora and fauna, with oak and chestnut forests, almond and cherry orchards, and wildflowers carpeting the landscape in a riot of color throughout the year.

Scenic viewpoints, natural springs, and picturesque waterfalls are scattered throughout the Alpujarras, providing opportunities for breathtaking vistas and peaceful moments of contemplation in nature.

3. Whitewashed Villages:

The Alpujarras is home to a collection of charming whitewashed villages, or "pueblos blancos," that cling to the mountainsides like clusters of pearls, each with its own unique character and charm.

Villages such as Pampaneira, Bubión, and Capileira are among the most picturesque in the region, with narrow cobblestone streets, traditional Moorish architecture, and terracotta rooftops that offer stunning views of the surrounding mountains and valleys.

Many of these villages have preserved their Moorish heritage and traditions, with artisan workshops, handicraft shops, and local markets selling handmade goods, pottery, and textiles produced by local artisans.

4. Cultural Heritage:

The Alpujarras region is rich in cultural heritage, with a legacy that reflects its Moorish, Christian, and Jewish influences.
Historic landmarks such as the Alpujarras Castle, the Church of San Juan Bautista, and the Moorish ruins of La Rábita are testament to the region's diverse history and architectural legacy.
Traditional festivals, music, and culinary traditions are celebrated throughout the year, offering visitors a glimpse into the vibrant cultural tapestry of the Alpujarras.

5. Outdoor Activities:

The Alpujarras region offers a wide range of outdoor activities for nature lovers and adventure seekers, including hiking, mountain biking, horseback riding, and birdwatching.

The region is crisscrossed by a network of well-marked hiking trails and footpaths that lead to scenic viewpoints, mountain peaks, and hidden valleys, allowing visitors to explore the natural beauty of the area at their own pace.

Adventure sports such as canyoning, rock climbing, and paragliding are also popular in the Alpujarras, with opportunities for adrenaline-pumping thrills amidst the stunning mountain scenery.

6. Culinary Delights:

The cuisine of the Alpujarras is a reflection of its rich agricultural heritage and diverse cultural influences, with dishes featuring locally sourced ingredients such as almonds, chestnuts, olive oil, and honey.

Traditional dishes such as "plato alpujarreño," a hearty meat and vegetable stew, and "torta alpujarreña," a sweet pastry filled with almonds and honey, are staples of the local gastronomy.
Visitors can sample these culinary delights at local restaurants, taverns, and mountain refuges, where they can enjoy authentic Andalusian cuisine in a rustic and welcoming atmosphere.

In summary, the Alpujarras region is a hidden gem waiting to be discovered, with its breathtaking landscapes, charming villages, and rich cultural heritage offering a unique and unforgettable experience for travelers seeking adventure, tranquility, and authenticity in the heart of Andalusia. Whether hiking through mountain trails, exploring ancient villages, or savoring local delicacies, a visit to the Alpujarras promises an immersive journey through the timeless beauty and enchanting traditions of southern Spain.

8.5 Villages Tour

Embarking on a villages tour in the Alpujarras region of southern Spain is like stepping back in time to a bygone era of Moorish influence, whitewashed buildings, and rustic charm. Nestled amidst the rugged mountains of the Sierra Nevada, these picturesque villages offer a glimpse into the rich cultural heritage and traditional way of life that has endured for centuries. From the narrow cobblestone streets and terraced hillsides to the quaint plazas and ancient architecture, each village has its own unique character and story to tell. Here's an extensive exploration of some of the most enchanting villages to include on your Alpujarras villages tour:

1. Pampaneira:

Pampaneira is one of the most picturesque villages in the Alpujarras, with its narrow winding streets, whitewashed houses, and stunning views of the surrounding mountains.
The village is known for its traditional Moorish architecture, artisan workshops, and handicraft shops, where visitors can browse handmade goods such as pottery, textiles, and leather goods.
Highlights of Pampaneira include the Church of Santa Cruz, the Ethnographic

Museum, and the Moorish-style fountain in the main square, Plaza de la Libertad.

2. Bubión:

Bubión is a charming hillside village perched on the slopes of the Sierra Nevada, offering panoramic views of the Poqueira Valley below.

The village is known for its traditional Alpujarran architecture, with flat-roofed houses, wooden balconies, and intricate stonework that reflects its Moorish heritage.

Visitors can explore the narrow streets of Bubión, visit the Church of San José, and enjoy a leisurely stroll through the village's terraced orchards and gardens.

3. Capileira:

Capileira is the highest and most scenic village in the Poqueira Valley, nestled beneath the towering peaks of the Sierra Nevada.

The village is famous for its traditional Alpujarran cuisine, with local specialties such as "plato alpujarreño" and "torta alpujarreña" served in cozy taverns and mountain restaurants.

Highlights of Capileira include the Church of Santa María la Mayor, the Moorish Quarter, and the scenic viewpoints overlooking the valley and surrounding mountains.

4. Trevelez:

Trevelez is the highest village in the Alpujarras and is renowned for its delicious cured hams, which are considered some of the best in Spain.

The village is divided into three distinct neighborhoods – Alto, Medio, and Bajo – each with its own unique architecture, traditions, and cultural heritage.

Visitors can explore the winding streets of Trevelez, visit the Church of San Benito, and sample the local cuisine at one of the village's many restaurants and tapas bars.

5. Lanjarón:

Lanjarón is a historic spa town known for its natural mineral springs, which have been attracting visitors for centuries with their reputed health benefits.
The town is famous for its annual water festival, held in June, which celebrates the healing properties of Lanjarón's springs with music, dancing, and traditional ceremonies.
Visitors can explore Lanjarón's charming streets, visit the Moorish Castle, and relax in the town's thermal baths and spa facilities.

6. Capileira:

Capileira is one of the most picturesque villages in the Alpujarras, with its whitewashed houses, narrow streets, and stunning views of the surrounding mountains.

The village is known for its traditional Moorish architecture, with flat-roofed houses, wooden balconies, and intricate stonework that reflects its rich cultural heritage.

Visitors can explore Capileira's winding streets, visit the Church of Santa María la Mayor, and enjoy panoramic views of the Poqueira Valley from the village's scenic viewpoints.

7. Pitres:

Pitres is a tranquil village located in the heart of the Alpujarras, surrounded by chestnut forests, olive groves, and fruit orchards.

The village is known for its traditional Alpujarran cuisine, with local specialties such as "olla de San Antón" and "migas" served in rustic taverns and family-run restaurants.

Highlights of Pitres include the Church of San Roque, the Ethnographic Museum, and the scenic trails that wind through the surrounding countryside.

8. Valor:

Valor is a small mountain village known for its breathtaking views, traditional architecture, and peaceful atmosphere.

The village is famous for its annual cherry festival, held in June, which celebrates the harvest of the region's delicious cherries with music, dancing, and culinary events.

Visitors can explore Valor's narrow streets, visit the Church of San Cristóbal, and hike the scenic trails that lead to nearby waterfalls and natural springs.

9. Ferreirola:

Ferreirola is a hidden gem nestled in the Taha Valley, surrounded by lush forests, meandering rivers, and dramatic mountain scenery.
The village is known for its traditional Alpujarran architecture, with whitewashed houses, flat-roofed buildings, and narrow cobblestone streets that wind through the village center.
Highlights of Ferreirola include the Church of San Juan Bautista, the Ethnographic Museum, and the scenic hiking trails that lead to nearby waterfalls and natural pools.

10. Busquistar:

Busquistar is a charming mountain village located in the heart of the Alpujarras, surrounded by terraced hillsides, ancient olive groves, and fruit orchards.

The village is known for its traditional Moorish architecture, with whitewashed houses, narrow streets, and stunning views of the surrounding mountains.

Visitors can explore Busquistar's historic center, visit the Church of San Antonio, and hike the scenic trails that wind through the surrounding countryside.

11. Safety and Tips:

When embarking on a villages tour in the Alpujarras, it's important to plan ahead, check the weather forecast, and wear appropriate footwear and clothing for hiking and outdoor exploration.

Many of the villages are connected by scenic hiking trails, allowing visitors to explore multiple villages in a single day and enjoy the natural beauty of the surrounding countryside.

Visitors should also respect the local customs and traditions of the villages they visit, including dressing modestly, asking permission before taking photographs of people or private property, and disposing of trash responsibly.

In summary, a villages tour in the Alpujarras offers a unique opportunity to explore the rich cultural heritage, stunning landscapes, and traditional way of life of this enchanting region of southern Spain. Whether wandering through ancient streets, sampling local cuisine, or simply soaking in the scenic beauty of the mountains, a visit to the Alpujarras villages promises an unforgettable journey through time and culture.

9.0 Cultural Immersion

9.1 Flamenco Shows

Flamenco, with its fiery passion, soul-stirring music, and mesmerizing dance, is one of Spain's most iconic cultural traditions. Originating from the Andalusian region, particularly in cities like Sevilla, Granada, and Córdoba, Flamenco is deeply rooted in Spanish history, culture, and identity. Attending a Flamenco show is an immersive experience that allows visitors to witness the raw emotion and artistry of this captivating art form. Here's an extensive exploration of Flamenco shows:

1. History and Origins:

Flamenco has a rich and complex history that traces its roots back to the cultural melting pot of Andalusia, where diverse influences from Moorish, Jewish, and Gypsy (Romani) communities converged.

The origins of Flamenco can be traced back to the 18th century, when it emerged as a form of artistic expression among marginalized communities in the Andalusian countryside.

Over the centuries, Flamenco evolved and diversified, incorporating elements of music, dance, song, and poetry to become the vibrant and dynamic art form that it is today.

2. Elements of Flamenco:

Flamenco is characterized by three main elements: cante (song), toque (guitar), and baile (dance), each of which contributes to the unique and expressive quality of the art form.

The cante, or Flamenco song, is characterized by its haunting melodies, soulful lyrics, and intense emotional expression, often accompanied by rhythmic clapping (palmas) and percussive footwork (zapateado).

The toque, or Flamenco guitar, provides the musical accompaniment for the cante and baile, with intricate melodies, rapid strumming patterns, and improvisational flourishes that complement the singer and dancer's performance.
The baile, or Flamenco dance, is the visual centerpiece of Flamenco performances, with dancers expressing a range of emotions – from joy and passion to sorrow and longing – through intricate footwork, dramatic gestures, and fluid movements of the body.

3. Flamenco Shows:

Flamenco shows, known as "tablaos," are held in intimate venues such as theaters, clubs, and restaurants, where audiences can experience the intensity and intimacy of Flamenco up close.

The performances typically feature a combination of cante, toque, and baile, with skilled musicians, singers, and dancers coming together to create a captivating and immersive experience.

Flamenco shows vary in style and format, ranging from traditional performances that adhere closely to Flamenco's roots to more contemporary interpretations that incorporate elements of fusion, jazz, and world music.

Some Flamenco shows also include opportunities for audience participation, with guests invited to join in the rhythmic clapping and foot stomping that are integral to Flamenco's rhythmic pulse.

4. Flamenco Venues:

In cities like Sevilla, Granada, and Córdoba, Flamenco shows can be found in a variety of venues, ranging from historic theaters and cultural centers to intimate taverns and flamenco clubs.

Tablaos, or Flamenco venues, often feature traditional Andalusian décor, with dim lighting, exposed brick walls, and rustic furnishings that create an intimate and authentic atmosphere.

Many Flamenco venues also offer dining options, allowing guests to enjoy a traditional Spanish meal or tapas before or after the performance, accompanied by regional wines and cocktails.

5. Tips for Attending Flamenco Shows:

It's recommended to book tickets for Flamenco shows in advance, especially during peak tourist seasons, to ensure availability and preferred seating.

Dressing in smart casual attire is appropriate for Flamenco shows, although some venues may have dress codes, so it's best to check in advance.

While Flamenco shows can be found throughout Andalusia, cities like Sevilla, Granada, and Córdoba are renowned for their vibrant Flamenco scenes, with numerous venues and performances to choose from.

Be prepared to immerse yourself in the passion and intensity of Flamenco, as the performances can be emotionally charged and deeply moving.

In summary, attending a Flamenco show in

Andalusia is a must-do experience for travelers seeking to immerse themselves in the rich cultural heritage and artistic traditions of Spain. From the soulful singing and virtuosic guitar playing to the mesmerizing dance and electrifying energy, Flamenco offers a window into the heart and soul of Spanish culture, leaving audiences spellbound and inspired by its timeless beauty and passion.

9.2 Tapas Tours

Tapas, the quintessential Spanish culinary tradition, offer a tantalizing array of small dishes bursting with flavor, creativity, and regional specialties. Originating from the custom of serving small snacks to accompany drinks, tapas have evolved into a vibrant and diverse culinary art form that showcases the rich gastronomic heritage of Spain. Embarking on a tapas tour is a delightful way to explore the local cuisine, culture, and traditions of Spain, one bite at a time. Here's an extensive exploration of tapas tours:

1. History and Origins of Tapas:

The history of tapas dates back centuries to the taverns and wine bars of Andalusia, where bartenders would cover glasses of wine with small plates or "tapas" to keep out dust and insects.

Over time, the custom of serving tapas evolved into a culinary tradition, with bars and restaurants across Spain offering a wide variety of small dishes to accompany drinks and socializing.

Today, tapas are enjoyed by people of all ages and backgrounds throughout Spain and have become synonymous with Spanish cuisine and conviviality.

2. Elements of a Tapas Tour:

A tapas tour typically involves visiting multiple bars, taverns, and restaurants in a specific neighborhood or city to sample a variety of tapas dishes and drinks.

Each stop on the tour offers a different culinary experience, with specialties ranging from traditional Spanish classics like jamón ibérico, tortilla española, and croquetas to regional specialties and modern interpretations of tapas.

In addition to tasting delicious food, participants of a tapas tour have the opportunity to learn about the history, culture, and culinary traditions of the region from knowledgeable guides and local experts.

3. Types of Tapas:

Tapas come in a wide variety of flavors, textures, and ingredients, reflecting the diverse culinary traditions of Spain's different regions and provinces.

Classic tapas dishes include patatas bravas (fried potatoes with spicy tomato sauce), gambas al ajillo (garlic shrimp), albondigas (meatballs), and pulpo a la gallega (Galician-style octopus).

Regional specialties may include pintxos from the Basque Country, montaditos from Andalusia, and pinchos morunos from Castilla-La Mancha, each offering a unique twist on the tapas tradition.

4. Tapas Tour Locations:

Tapas tours can be found in cities and towns throughout Spain, with popular destinations including Madrid, Barcelona, Sevilla, Granada, and San Sebastián.

In larger cities, tapas tours may focus on specific neighborhoods or districts known for their culinary offerings, such as the historic center of Sevilla or the trendy El Born district in Barcelona.

In smaller towns and villages, tapas tours may highlight local specialties and traditional dishes unique to the region, providing a taste of authentic Spanish cuisine and culture.

5. Tips for Enjoying a Tapas Tour:

When participating in a tapas tour, it's important to pace yourself and savor each dish, as the experience is as much about enjoying the food as it is about socializing and exploring.

Be open to trying new flavors and ingredients, as tapas offer a wide variety of options for every palate, from savory meats and cheeses to fresh seafood and seasonal produce.

Engage with your guide and fellow tour participants, as they can offer valuable insights and recommendations for the best tapas bars and dishes in the area.

Take the opportunity to learn about the history, culture, and culinary traditions of Spain from your guide, who can provide fascinating insights into the stories behind the food and drink you're enjoying.

In summary, a tapas tour offers a delicious and immersive way to experience the vibrant flavors, rich culinary heritage, and convivial atmosphere of Spanish cuisine. Whether sampling classic tapas dishes in Madrid, exploring regional specialties in Andalusia, or indulging in pintxos in the

Basque Country, a tapas tour promises an unforgettable culinary journey through the heart and soul of Spain.

9.3 Local Festivals

Spain is renowned for its vibrant and colorful festivals, which celebrate a rich tapestry of cultural traditions, religious heritage, and community spirit. From lively street parades and flamboyant costumes to traditional music and dance, each festival offers a unique opportunity to immerse oneself in the vibrant culture and heritage of Spain. Here's an extensive exploration of some of the most iconic local festivals across the country:

1. La Tomatina (Buñol, Valencia):

La Tomatina is perhaps one of the most famous and unconventional festivals in Spain, held annually in the small town of Buñol, Valencia.

The festival involves a massive tomato fight, where participants from around the world gather to throw ripe tomatoes at each other in a playful and chaotic battle.

La Tomatina attracts thousands of visitors each year and has become a symbol of Spain's fun-loving and adventurous spirit.

2. Feria de Abril (Sevilla, Andalusia):

The Feria de Abril is a week-long festival held in the Andalusian city of Sevilla, celebrating the region's cultural heritage, music, and dance.

The festival features colorful casetas (marquee tents) set up along the banks of the Guadalquivir River, where locals and visitors gather to dance sevillanas, enjoy traditional Andalusian cuisine, and socialize with friends and family.

Flamenco performances, horse parades, and bullfights are also highlights of the Feria de Abril, making it a must-visit event for anyone interested in experiencing the vibrant culture of southern Spain.

3. San Fermín (Pamplona, Navarre):

San Fermín is a world-famous festival held in the city of Pamplona, Navarre, known for its iconic "encierro" or running of the bulls.

The festival begins with the "chupinazo," a ceremonial rocket launch that marks the start of the festivities, followed by a week of bull runs, street parties, and cultural events.

While the running of the bulls is the most well-known aspect of San Fermín, the festival also includes traditional music, dance, and religious ceremonies that pay homage to the city's patron saint.

4. Carnival (Tenerife, Canary Islands):

Carnival is celebrated with great fervor and enthusiasm throughout Spain, but the Carnival of Santa Cruz de Tenerife in the Canary Islands is one of the largest and most spectacular in the country.

The festival features colorful parades, elaborate costumes, and lively street parties that attract thousands of visitors from around the world.

Highlights of the Carnival of Tenerife include the crowning of the Carnival Queen, the burial of the sardine, and the traditional "murgas" and "comparsas" performances, which showcase the island's rich musical and theatrical traditions.

5. Semana Santa (Various Cities):

Semana Santa, or Holy Week, is one of the most important religious festivals in Spain, observed with solemn processions, religious ceremonies, and elaborate floats depicting scenes from the Passion of Christ.

Cities such as Sevilla, Granada, and Málaga are renowned for their Semana Santa celebrations, which attract thousands of pilgrims and spectators each year.

The processions are accompanied by haunting music, incense-filled streets, and the rhythmic sound of drumbeats, creating a solemn and atmospheric experience for participants and observers alike.

6. Tips for Enjoying Local Festivals:

Plan ahead and research the dates, locations, and activities of the festival you wish to attend, as many festivals are held annually and may require advance booking for accommodations and transportation.

Arrive early to secure a good spot for viewing parades and performances, especially for popular events like La Tomatina or San Fermín.

Respect local customs and traditions, including dress codes, photography etiquette, and religious practices, to ensure a respectful and enjoyable experience for yourself and others.

Be prepared for large crowds, loud music, and long hours of festivities, as many festivals in Spain last for several days and nights.

In summary, local festivals offer a unique opportunity to experience the vibrant culture, rich traditions, and festive spirit of Spain. Whether participating in the tomato-throwing madness of La Tomatina, dancing the night away at the Feria de Abril, or witnessing the solemn processions of Semana Santa, attending a local festival promises an unforgettable journey through the heart and soul of Spanish culture.

10.0 Practical Tips

10.1 Language and Communication

Language and communication are the cornerstones of human interaction, facilitating the exchange of ideas, emotions, and information across cultures, societies, and generations. From spoken words and written texts to nonverbal cues and gestures, language encompasses a rich and diverse array of forms and expressions that shape our understanding of the world and our relationships with others. Here's an extensive exploration of language and communication:

1. The Nature of Language:

Language is a complex and multifaceted system of communication that allows individuals to convey thoughts, feelings, and intentions through a structured set of symbols, sounds, and rules.

Human languages vary widely in their structure, vocabulary, and grammar, reflecting the diverse cultures, histories, and geographies of the societies that use them.

Linguists study language from various perspectives, including phonetics (the study of speech sounds), syntax (the study of sentence structure), semantics (the study of meaning), and pragmatics (the study of language in context).

2. Forms of Communication:

Communication encompasses a broad range of modalities beyond spoken and written language, including nonverbal communication, visual communication, and digital communication.

Nonverbal communication involves gestures, facial expressions, body language, and eye contact, which can convey meaning and emotions without the use of words.

Visual communication utilizes images, symbols, and visual elements to convey information and ideas, as seen in signage, graphic design, and multimedia presentations.

Digital communication encompasses various forms of electronic communication, including email, social media, instant messaging, and video conferencing, which have transformed the way people connect and interact in the modern world.

3. Language Acquisition and Development:

Language acquisition refers to the process by which individuals learn and internalize a language, typically beginning in early childhood through exposure to caregivers, family members, and the surrounding environment.

Children acquire language skills gradually, starting with babbling and simple words before progressing to more complex sentences and linguistic structures.

Language development is influenced by various factors, including genetics, environment, culture, and social interactions, shaping individuals' linguistic abilities and communication styles throughout their lives.

4. Multilingualism and Language Diversity:

Multilingualism refers to the ability to speak multiple languages fluently, a common phenomenon in many parts of the world where people are exposed to different linguistic and cultural influences.

Language diversity is a hallmark of human society, with thousands of languages spoken around the globe, each reflecting the unique histories, identities, and worldviews of the communities that use them.

Language revitalization efforts aim to preserve and promote endangered languages threatened by cultural assimilation, globalization, and language shift, recognizing the intrinsic value of linguistic diversity to human culture and heritage.

5. The Power of Communication:

Effective communication is essential for building relationships, fostering understanding, and resolving conflicts in personal, professional, and social contexts. Communication skills, including active listening, empathy, and clarity of expression, are valued attributes that contribute to success in various domains, such as education, business, diplomacy, and interpersonal relationships.

Miscommunication and misunderstandings can arise from linguistic differences, cultural differences, and contextual factors, highlighting the importance of clear and respectful communication practices in diverse and multicultural environments.

6. Language and Identity:

Language plays a central role in shaping individual and collective identities, providing a sense of belonging, heritage, and cultural continuity for speakers of a particular language.

Language can also be a marker of social status, power, and privilege, with certain languages and dialects being associated with prestige or marginalization within society.

Language revitalization and preservation efforts are often motivated by a desire to reclaim and celebrate linguistic heritage, strengthen cultural identity, and foster a sense of pride and solidarity among language communities.

7. Technology and Language:

Advances in technology have revolutionized language and communication, enabling instant global connectivity and facilitating the exchange of information and ideas across linguistic and cultural boundaries.
Translation and interpretation technologies, such as machine translation, speech recognition, and language learning apps, have made it easier for individuals to communicate and interact in multilingual environments.
However, technology also presents challenges in terms of language

preservation, linguistic accuracy, and digital literacy, raising questions about the future of language and communication in the digital age.

8. Basic Granada phrases

Visiting Granada, with its rich history, vibrant culture, and warm-hearted locals, presents an excellent opportunity to immerse yourself in the local language and connect more deeply with the community. Whether you're exploring the enchanting Alhambra, wandering through the narrow streets of the Albayzín, or savoring tapas in bustling taverns, mastering some basic Granada phrases will enhance your experience and make your interactions more enjoyable. Here's an extensive guide to basic Granada phrases:

A. Greetings and Pleasantries:

"Hola" (OH-lah) - Hello

"Buenos días" (BWEH-nos DEE-ahs) - Good morning

"Buenas tardes" (BWEH-nas TAR-des) - Good afternoon

"Buenas noches" (BWEH-nas NO-chehs) - Good evening / Good night

"¿Cómo estás?" (KOH-moh ehs-TAHS) - How are you? (informal)

"¿Cómo está usted?" (KOH-moh ehs-TAH oos-TEHD) - How are you? (formal)

"Bien, gracias. ¿Y tú?" (BYEN, GRAH-syahs. EE too?) - Fine, thank you. And you? (informal)

"Muy bien, gracias. ¿Y usted?" (MWEY BYEN, GRAH-syahs. EE oos-TEHD?) - Very well, thank you. And you? (formal)

"Hasta luego" (AH-stah LWEH-goh) - See you later

"Adiós" (ah-DYOHS) - Goodbye

B. Asking for Help and Directions:

"¿Dónde está...?" (DOHN-deh ehs-TAH...?) - Where is...?

"¿Cómo llego a...?" (KOH-moh YEH-goh ah...?) - How do I get to...?

"¿Puede ayudarme, por favor?" (PWEH-deh ah-yoo-DAHR-meh, por fah-VOHR?) - Can you help me, please?

"¿Habla inglés?" (AH-blah een-GLAYS?) - Do you speak English?

"No entiendo" (noh ehn-TYEHN-doh) - I don't understand

"¿Cuánto cuesta?" (KWAHN-toh KWEHS-tah?) - How much does it cost?

"¿Podría repetirlo, por favor?" (poh-DREE-ah reh-peh-TEER-loh, por fah-VOHR?) - Could you repeat that, please?

C. Ordering Food and Drinks:

"Una cerveza, por favor" (OO-nah sehr-BEH-sah, por fah-VOHR) - A beer, please

"Una copa de vino tinto/blanco, por favor" (OO-nah KOH-pah deh BEE-noh TEEN-toh/BLAHN-koh, por fah-VOHR) - A glass of red/white wine, please

"Quisiera un café con leche" (kee-SYE-rah oon kah-FEH kon LEH-cheh) - I would like a coffee with milk

"¿Qué recomienda?" (keh reh-koh-myen-dah?) - What do you recommend?

"La cuenta, por favor" (lah KWEHN-tah, por fah-VOHR) - The bill, please

D. Expressing Gratitude:

"Gracias" (GRAH-syahs) - Thank you
"Muchas gracias" (MOO-chahs GRAH-syahs) - Thank you very much
"De nada" (deh NAH-dah) - You're welcome

"Por favor" (por fah-VOHR) - Please

E. Making Small Talk:

"¿De dónde eres?" (deh DOHN-deh EH-rehs?) - Where are you from?
"¿Cuánto tiempo llevas aquí?" (KWAHN-toh tee-EM-poh YEH-bahs ah-KEE?) - How long have you been here?
"¿Te gusta Granada?" (teh GOOS-tah grah-NAH-dah?) - Do you like Granada?
"¿Has estado en la Alhambra?" (ahs ehs-TAH-doh en lah ahl-ahm-BRAH?) - Have you been to the Alhambra?
"¿Cuál es tu lugar favorito en Granada?" (KWAHL ehs too LWAHR fah-boh-REE-toh en grah-NAH-dah?) - What's your favorite place in Granada?

F. Understanding Common Expressions:

"Vale" (VAH-leh) - Okay / All right

"Sí" (SEE) - Yes
"No" (NOH) - No
"Por supuesto" (por soo-PWEHS-toh) - Of course
"Lo siento" (loh SYEHN-toh) - I'm sorry

G. Showing Excitement:

"¡Qué emocionante!" (keh eh-moh-thyo-NAHN-teh) - How exciting!
"¡Qué maravilloso!" (keh mah-rah-bee-YOH-soh) - How marvelous!
"¡Qué hermoso!" (keh ehr-MOH-soh) - How beautiful!

H. Expressing Agreement and Disagreement:

"Sí, claro" (SEE, KLAH-roh) - Yes, of course
"No estoy de acuerdo" (noh ehs-TOY deh ah-KWEHR-doh) - I don't agree

"Tienes razón" (TYEH-nes rah-THYOHN) - You're right

"No sé" (noh say) - I don't know

I. Seeking Clarification:

"¿Puede hablar más despacio, por favor?" (PWEH-deh ah-BLAHR mah dehs-PAH-thyo, por fah-VOHR?) - Can you speak more slowly, please?

"¿Qué significa esto?" (keh see-NEE-fee-kah EHS-toh?) - What does this mean?

J. Navigating Social Situations:

"Perdón" (pehr-DOHN) - Excuse me / I'm sorry

"Con permiso" (kohn pehr-MEE-soh

In summary, language and communication are fundamental aspects of human existence, shaping our interactions, perceptions, and experiences in profound ways. From the spoken word to the written text, from nonverbal cues to digital messages, language encompasses a rich tapestry of forms and expressions that reflect the diversity and complexity of human culture and society. Understanding and appreciating the power of language and communication is essential for navigating the complexities of the modern world and building meaningful connections with others across linguistic and cultural divides.

10.2 Photography Etiquette

Photography is a powerful medium for preserving memories, documenting experiences, and expressing creativity. However, it's essential to approach photography with respect, especially when capturing images of people, places, and cultures. Photography etiquette encompasses a set of principles and guidelines designed to ensure that photographers conduct themselves ethically, responsibly, and considerately. Whether you're a professional photographer or an amateur enthusiast, here's an extensive guide to photography etiquette:

1. Respect Privacy:

Always ask for permission before taking photographs of individuals, particularly in private or intimate settings.

Be mindful of people's personal space and cultural sensitivities when photographing in public spaces or crowded areas.

Avoid photographing individuals without their consent, especially in situations where they may feel uncomfortable or vulnerable.

2. Obtain Consent:

When photographing people, especially strangers, seek their consent before taking their picture.

Explain the purpose of the photograph and how it will be used, whether for personal enjoyment, artistic expression, or publication.

Respect people's right to decline being photographed or to request that their image not be shared publicly.

3. Be Discreet:

Use discretion when photographing sensitive or private moments, such as religious ceremonies, funerals, or personal interactions.

Avoid intruding on people's personal space or interrupting their activities for the sake of a photograph.

Be aware of your surroundings and consider how your presence and actions may affect the subjects you're photographing.

4. Cultural Sensitivity:

Familiarize yourself with the cultural norms and customs of the places you're photographing, especially when traveling to foreign countries or communities with different traditions.

Respect sacred sites, cultural artifacts, and religious practices by adhering to any photography restrictions or guidelines set by local authorities or community leaders.

Exercise sensitivity and discretion when photographing individuals from diverse cultural backgrounds, taking care to avoid stereotypes or misrepresentations.

5. Protect the Environment:

Practice environmental stewardship by minimizing your impact on natural habitats and ecosystems when photographing outdoors.
Avoid trampling on vegetation, disturbing wildlife, or leaving behind litter or debris while exploring natural landscapes.
Follow Leave No Trace principles and adhere to any regulations or guidelines governing photography in protected areas, national parks, or wildlife reserves.

6. Respect Property Rights:

Obtain permission from property owners or authorities before photographing on private property, commercial premises, or restricted areas.

Respect signage, barriers, and designated photography zones that indicate where photography is permitted or prohibited.

Refrain from trespassing or entering restricted areas to capture photographs without proper authorization.

7. Practice Ethical Editing:

Use photo editing software responsibly, avoiding excessive manipulation or alterations that misrepresent reality or deceive viewers.

Disclose any significant edits or enhancements made to your photographs, especially if they alter the factual accuracy or integrity of the image.

Respect the original intent and integrity of the subjects you photograph by representing them truthfully and authentically in your images.

8. Be Courteous to Other Photographers:

Show consideration for fellow photographers by avoiding obstructing their view or interfering with their shots in crowded or popular photography locations.
Practice patience and cooperation when sharing photography spaces, especially during events, festivals, or tourist attractions where multiple photographers may be present.
Foster a sense of camaraderie and mutual respect among photographers by offering assistance, sharing tips, and collaborating on creative projects.

9. Practice Safe and Responsible Photography:

Prioritize safety when photographing in challenging or hazardous environments, such as rugged terrain, extreme weather conditions, or high-traffic areas.
Follow safety guidelines and exercise caution when using photography equipment, especially when working with tripods, drones, or other accessories that may pose risks to yourself or others.
Respect local laws, regulations, and ethical standards governing photography, and seek appropriate permits or permissions when required for specific photography activities or projects.

10. Share Your Passion Responsibly:

Share your photographs thoughtfully and responsibly on social media, photo-sharing platforms, or personal websites, considering the potential impact of your images on viewers and subjects alike.

Provide context, captions, or credits when sharing photographs online to give proper attribution to the subjects, locations, or events depicted in your images.

Use your photography as a tool for positive change, advocacy, and social awareness by highlighting important issues, promoting diversity, and amplifying marginalized voices through your work.

By adhering to these principles of photography etiquette, photographers can cultivate a respectful and ethical approach to their craft, fostering meaningful connections with their subjects and contributing to a culture of integrity, empathy, and creativity within the photography community and beyond.

10.3 General emergency contact in Granada

When traveling to Granada or any unfamiliar destination, it's essential to be prepared for unexpected emergencies. Knowing who to contact in case of an emergency can provide peace of mind and ensure prompt assistance when needed. Whether you're facing a medical crisis, a safety concern, or a natural disaster, having access to general emergency contacts in Granada can make all the difference. Here's an extensive guide to essential emergency contacts in Granada:

1. Emergency Services:

Emergency Number:
Dial: 112
Description: The emergency number 112 is the universal emergency services hotline in Spain, including Granada. It operates 24/7 and provides access to police, fire, medical, and rescue services. When you dial 112, trained operators will assess your situation and dispatch the appropriate emergency response teams to assist you.

2. Medical Emergencies:

Ambulance / Medical Emergency Services:
Dial: 112
Description: If you or someone else requires urgent medical attention due to illness, injury, or medical crisis, dialing 112 will connect you to medical emergency services. Trained paramedics and medical professionals will respond promptly to assess and treat the patient and transport

them to the nearest hospital or medical facility if necessary.

Hospital Emergency Departments:

Hospital Universitario San Cecilio:

Address: Av. Doctor Olóriz, 16, 18012 Granada, Spain

Phone: +34 958 02 42 52

Hospital Virgen de las Nieves:

Address: Av. de las Fuerzas Armadas, 2, 18014 Granada, Spain

Phone: +34 958 02 40 00

Pharmacies:

In non-emergency situations, you can locate nearby pharmacies using online maps or directories. Pharmacies in Granada typically operate during regular business hours, but some may offer emergency services or after-hours assistance on a rotating basis.

3. Police and Law Enforcement:

Local Police:

Dial: 092

Description: For non-emergency situations requiring police assistance, such as reporting theft, vandalism, or disturbances, you can dial the local police number 092. Local police officers are responsible for maintaining public order, enforcing local laws, and providing assistance to residents and visitors in Granada.

National Police:

Dial: 091

Description: The national police number 091 is another option for contacting law enforcement authorities in Granada. National police officers handle a wide range of law enforcement duties, including criminal investigations, border security, and counter-terrorism efforts.

4. Fire and Rescue Services:

Fire Department:

Dial: 112

Description: In the event of a fire, explosion, or other emergencies requiring fire and rescue services, dialing 112 will connect you to the nearest fire department. Highly trained firefighters equipped with specialized equipment will respond to the scene to extinguish fires, conduct rescue operations, and provide assistance to those affected by the emergency.

5. Consular Services:

Consulate General of the United States in Barcelona:
Address: Paseo Reina Elisenda de Montcada, 23, 08034 Barcelona, Spain
Phone: +34 932 80 33 22
Email: BarcelonaACS@state.gov
Description: For travelers from the United States requiring consular assistance, including assistance with lost passports,

medical emergencies, or legal issues, the Consulate General of the United States in Barcelona provides consular services to U.S. citizens in Granada and the surrounding region.

6. Roadside Assistance:

Roadside Assistance:
Dial: 112
Description: If you experience car trouble, breakdowns, or accidents while driving in Granada, you can call 112 for roadside assistance. Trained personnel will provide assistance, towing services, or other forms of support to help you safely resolve the situation and get back on the road.

7. Tourist Assistance:

Tourist Information Office:

Address: Plaza del Carmen, 4, 18009 Granada, Spain
Phone: +34 958 24 70 15
Description: The Tourist Information Office in Granada provides assistance to visitors, including information on local attractions, transportation options, accommodations, and emergency services. Staffed by multilingual professionals, the office can offer guidance and support to tourists in need of assistance.

By familiarizing yourself with these general emergency contacts in Granada and keeping them readily accessible, you can better prepare for unforeseen circumstances and respond effectively to emergencies while traveling in this beautiful city. Remember that prompt action and clear communication are key to ensuring your safety and well-being in any emergency situation.

11.0 Sample Itineraries

11.1 One Week Itinerary

Granada, with its rich history, stunning architecture, vibrant culture, and breathtaking natural landscapes, offers an unforgettable experience for travelers seeking to immerse themselves in the beauty and charm of southern Spain. Planning a one-week itinerary allows you to explore the city's iconic landmarks, indulge in local cuisine, and venture into the surrounding countryside for outdoor adventures. Here's an extensive guide to crafting your perfect one-week itinerary in Granada:

Day 1: Arrival and Orientation

Morning:

Arrive in Granada and check into your accommodation.
Enjoy a leisurely breakfast at a local café or bakery.

Afternoon:
Take a walking tour of the city center, starting at Plaza Nueva and exploring the historic streets of the Albayzín neighborhood.
Visit the Mirador de San Nicolás for panoramic views of the Alhambra and the Sierra Nevada mountains.

Evening:
Sample traditional tapas at one of the many tapas bars in the Albayzín or Realejo neighborhoods.
Stroll through the lively streets of Calle Elvira and Plaza Bib-Rambla, soaking in the atmosphere of Granada's nightlife.

Day 2: Explore the Alhambra

Morning:
Reserve tickets in advance to visit the Alhambra, the UNESCO World Heritage site and the crown jewel of Granada.
Explore the Nasrid Palaces, Generalife Gardens, and Alcazaba Fortress within the Alhambra complex.

Afternoon:
Enjoy a leisurely lunch at one of the on-site cafes or restaurants.
Visit the Museum of Alhambra to learn more about the history and significance of this iconic monument.

Evening:
Relax and unwind with a flamenco show in the Sacromonte neighborhood, known for its cave dwellings and vibrant flamenco scene.

Day 3: Cultural Immersion

Morning:
Visit the Granada Cathedral, a masterpiece of Spanish Renaissance architecture, and explore its magnificent interior.
Wander through the Alcaicería, the historic Moorish silk market, now home to shops selling local crafts and souvenirs.

Afternoon:
Explore the historic district of Realejo, known for its narrow streets, historic buildings, and charming squares.
Visit the Casa de los Tiros, a 16th-century palace-turned-museum showcasing Granada's cultural heritage.

Evening:
Dine at a traditional Andalusian restaurant and savor regional specialties such as paella, gazpacho, and piononos.

Day 4: Day Trip to Sierra Nevada

Morning:
Take a day trip to the Sierra Nevada National Park, located just a short drive from Granada.
Explore the mountain villages of Capileira, Pampaneira, and Bubión, known for their whitewashed houses and stunning views.

Afternoon:
Hike one of the many scenic trails in the Sierra Nevada, ranging from easy walks to challenging mountain climbs.
Enjoy a picnic lunch surrounded by the natural beauty of the park.

Evening:
Return to Granada and relax with a spa treatment or massage at one of the city's wellness centers.

Day 5: Culinary Delights

Morning:
Take a cooking class to learn how to prepare traditional Andalusian dishes such as paella, gazpacho, and tapas.
Visit the local market to shop for fresh ingredients and sample regional specialties.

Afternoon:
Enjoy a leisurely lunch at a traditional tavern or bodega, where you can savor a variety of tapas and local wines.
Explore the Realejo neighborhood and discover hidden gems such as artisanal bakeries and gourmet food shops.

Evening:
Join a tapas tour to experience the best of Granada's culinary scene, sampling a variety of dishes at multiple restaurants and bars.

Day 6: Day Trip to the Alpujarras

Morning:
Take a scenic drive to the Alpujarras, a picturesque region known for its whitewashed villages, terraced hillsides, and stunning mountain scenery.
Explore the villages of Pampaneira, Bubión, and Capileira, stopping to admire the Moorish architecture and enjoy the local hospitality.

Afternoon:
Visit a local artisan workshop to learn about traditional crafts such as pottery, weaving, and woodcarving.
Enjoy a traditional lunch at a local restaurant, featuring fresh ingredients and regional specialties.

Evening:

Return to Granada and relax with a stroll along the Paseo de los Tristes, a scenic riverside promenade lined with cafes and bars.

Day 7: Relaxation and Reflection

Morning:
Spend the morning exploring the historic streets of the Albayzín, taking in the views of the Alhambra and the surrounding countryside.
Visit the Hammam Al Ándalus, a traditional Arab bathhouse, for a relaxing spa experience.

Afternoon:
Enjoy a leisurely lunch at a rooftop terrace restaurant, with panoramic views of the city and the mountains.
Take a siesta or relax in one of the city's parks or gardens, such as the Parque

Federico García Lorca or the Jardines del Triunfo.

Evening:
Reflect on your week in Granada over a glass of wine or a cup of tea at a local cafe, savoring the memories of your unforgettable journey.

By following this extensive one-week itinerary, you'll have the opportunity to explore the best of Granada's cultural heritage, natural beauty, and culinary delights, creating memories that will last a lifetime. Adjust the itinerary to suit your interests, preferences, and travel style, and don't forget to leave room for spontaneity and unexpected discoveries along the way. Whether you're a history buff, a foodie, an outdoor enthusiast, or a culture seeker, Granada has something to offer for every traveler.

11.2 Weekend Getaway

Granada, nestled in the heart of Andalusia, Spain, is an ideal destination for a weekend getaway filled with rich history, vibrant culture, and stunning landscapes. Whether you're seeking a romantic escape, a cultural adventure, or a relaxing break from the hustle and bustle of daily life, Granada offers a perfect blend of experiences to rejuvenate and inspire. Here's an extensive guide to planning your weekend getaway to Granada:

Day 1: Arrival and Exploration

Morning:

Arrive in Granada and check into your chosen accommodation, whether it's a luxurious hotel, a cozy boutique guesthouse, or a charming Airbnb.

Enjoy a leisurely breakfast at a local café or bakery, savoring freshly baked pastries and aromatic coffee.

Afternoon:

Start your exploration of Granada by wandering through the historic streets of the Albayzín neighborhood, a UNESCO World Heritage site known for its Moorish architecture and labyrinthine alleys.

Visit the Mirador de San Nicolás for breathtaking views of the Alhambra Palace and the Sierra Nevada mountains.

Evening:

Experience the magic of a flamenco show in the Sacromonte neighborhood, where you can immerse yourself in the passionate rhythms and soulful melodies of this traditional Spanish art form.

Indulge in a delicious dinner at a local restaurant, sampling Andalusian specialties such as gazpacho, paella, and tapas.

Day 2: Discovering the Alhambra

Morning:
Reserve tickets in advance to visit the Alhambra, the crown jewel of Granada and one of Spain's most iconic landmarks.

Explore the Nasrid Palaces, Generalife Gardens, and Alcazaba Fortress within the Alhambra complex, marveling at the intricate Moorish architecture and exquisite gardens.

Afternoon:
Enjoy a leisurely lunch at one of the on-site cafes or restaurants, savoring traditional

Spanish dishes with a backdrop of stunning views.

Visit the nearby Albayzín district and explore its historic streets, ancient mosques, and charming plazas, stopping to admire the views of the Alhambra from different vantage points.

Evening:
Relax and unwind with a stroll along the Paseo de los Tristes, a scenic riverside promenade lined with cafes and bars.

Dine at a rooftop terrace restaurant, where you can enjoy panoramic views of the city while savoring delicious Spanish cuisine and local wines.

Day 3: Cultural Immersion and Farewell

Morning:
Visit the Granada Cathedral, a masterpiece of Spanish Renaissance architecture, and

explore its magnificent interior, including the Royal Chapel and the crypt of the Catholic Monarchs.

Wander through the Alcaicería, the historic Moorish silk market, now home to shops selling local crafts and souvenirs.

Afternoon:

Take a guided tour of the historic Albaicín neighborhood, learning about its fascinating history, cultural heritage, and architectural landmarks.

Visit the Museum of Alhambra to delve deeper into the history and significance of the Alhambra Palace and its role in shaping Granada's identity.

Evening:

Enjoy a farewell dinner at a traditional Andalusian restaurant, savoring the flavors of regional cuisine and toasting to the memories of your weekend getaway.

Reflect on your time in Granada, soaking in the ambiance of the city's historic streets and vibrant culture.

Additional Tips:

Transportation: Granada is easily accessible by train, bus, or car from major cities in Spain, such as Madrid, Barcelona, and Seville. Once in Granada, you can explore the city on foot, by public transportation, or by taxi.

Accommodation: Choose accommodation that suits your preferences and budget, whether it's a luxury hotel in the city center, a charming guesthouse in the Albayzín, or a cozy apartment in the historic district.

Reservations: Make advance reservations for popular attractions, restaurants, and activities to ensure availability and avoid long queues or disappointment.

Local Cuisine: Don't miss the opportunity to sample Andalusian specialties such as tapas, paella, gazpacho, and piononos, as well as local wines, sherries, and cocktails.

Cultural Experiences: Immerse yourself in Granada's rich cultural heritage by attending a flamenco show, visiting historic landmarks, exploring traditional markets, and participating in guided tours and cultural activities.

By following this extensive guide, you can make the most of your weekend getaway to Granada, immersing yourself in the city's captivating beauty, history, and culture. Whether you're exploring ancient palaces, savoring local cuisine, or simply soaking in the ambiance of the city's historic streets,

Granada promises an unforgettable experience that will leave you feeling refreshed, inspired, and longing to return.

11.3 Budget Traveler's Guide

Granada, with its rich history, stunning architecture, and vibrant culture, is a city that offers plenty of opportunities for budget-conscious travelers to explore and enjoy. From affordable accommodations and budget-friendly dining options to free attractions and local experiences, Granada welcomes travelers of all budgets with open arms. Here's an extensive guide to help you make the most of your budget-friendly adventure in Granada:

1. Accommodation:

Hostels and Guesthouses: Granada offers a variety of budget-friendly hostels and guesthouses, where you can find dormitory beds or private rooms at affordable rates. Look for options in the Albayzín, Realejo, or Centro neighborhoods for convenient access to attractions and amenities.

Airbnb: Consider renting a room or apartment through Airbnb, which can often be more budget-friendly than traditional hotels. Look for accommodations in residential areas for a more authentic local experience.

Camping: If you're traveling during the warmer months, camping can be a budget-friendly option. There are campsites located just outside of Granada, offering basic facilities and beautiful natural surroundings.

2. Dining:

Tapas Bars: Take advantage of Granada's tapas culture, where you can enjoy a free tapa with every drink purchase at many bars and restaurants. Look for local establishments in the Albayzín, Realejo, and Centro neighborhoods for the best deals.

Menu del Día: Many restaurants offer a fixed-price menu del día (menu of the day) during lunchtime, which typically includes a starter, main course, dessert, and drink at a reasonable price.

Supermarkets and Markets: Save money by shopping for groceries at supermarkets and local markets, where you can find fresh produce, bread, cheese, and other essentials for picnics or simple meals.

3. Transportation:

Walking: Granada's compact size and pedestrian-friendly streets make it easy to explore on foot. Many of the city's main attractions are within walking distance of each other, allowing you to save money on transportation.

Public Transportation: Granada has an extensive public transportation network, including buses and trams, which can be an affordable option for getting around the city and surrounding areas. Consider purchasing a rechargeable transport card for discounted fares.

Bike Rentals: Renting a bike can be a fun and cost-effective way to explore Granada. Look for bike rental shops in the city center or consider using the city's bike-sharing program for short trips.

4. Attractions and Activities:

Free Attractions: Take advantage of Granada's many free attractions, including the Albaicín neighborhood, the Mirador de San Nicolás, and the Plaza Bib-Rambla. Explore the city's historic streets, visit local parks and gardens, and admire the stunning views of the Alhambra from various vantage points.

Discounted Tickets: Look for discounted tickets or combination passes for paid attractions such as the Alhambra, the Cathedral, and the Science Park. Many attractions offer reduced rates for students, seniors, and EU residents, so be sure to inquire about discounts.

Outdoor Activities: Enjoy outdoor activities such as hiking, picnicking, and sightseeing in the surrounding countryside and natural parks, including the Sierra Nevada National Park and the Alpujarras region.

5. Entertainment and Nightlife:

Free Events: Keep an eye out for free events and cultural activities happening around Granada, such as street performances, live music concerts, and art exhibitions. Check local listings and event calendars for upcoming events.

BYOB: Save money on drinks by purchasing beverages from supermarkets or local liquor stores and enjoying them in public spaces or at your accommodation before heading out for the evening.

Happy Hour Specials: Take advantage of happy hour specials and drink promotions offered by bars and clubs in Granada. Look for establishments that offer discounted drinks during certain hours of the day or week.

6. Local Tips:

Timing: Visit popular attractions early in the morning or late in the afternoon to avoid crowds and take advantage of quieter times.
Water: Carry a reusable water bottle and refill it at public drinking fountains or taps to save money on bottled water.

Language: Learn a few basic Spanish phrases to communicate with locals and navigate daily interactions more easily.

By following this extensive guide, budget travelers can explore Granada's beauty, culture, and charm without breaking the bank. With careful planning, savvy choices, and a spirit of adventure, you can make the most of your budget-friendly adventure in this captivating city.

12.0 Conclusion

Granada is a city that captivates the heart and soul of every traveler with its rich history, breathtaking landscapes, and vibrant culture. From the majestic Alhambra Palace to the charming streets of the Albayzín, Granada offers a treasure trove of experiences waiting to be discovered. Whether you're wandering through ancient Moorish palaces, savoring tapas in lively neighborhood bars, or gazing at the snow-capped peaks of the Sierra Nevada mountains, every moment in Granada is infused with beauty, wonder, and enchantment.

As you embark on your journey to Granada, may this travel guide serve as your trusted companion, guiding you through the city's hidden gems, local secrets, and unforgettable adventures. Whether you're a history buff, a food lover, a nature enthusiast, or an art aficionado, Granada welcomes you with open arms, inviting you to immerse yourself in its rich tapestry of sights, sounds, and flavors.

So pack your bags, lace up your shoes, and prepare to embark on the adventure of a lifetime in Granada. Whether you spend a weekend exploring its historic landmarks or a week delving into its hidden corners, one thing is certain: Granada will leave an indelible mark on your heart, beckoning you back time and time again to uncover its endless treasures and create memories that will last a lifetime. As the saying goes, "Quien no ha visto Granada, no ha visto nada" – "He who has not seen Granada, has seen nothing." So come and experience the magic of Granada for yourself – you won't be disappointed.

Printed in Great Britain
by Amazon